WHITE WATER, BEARS,
DRY FLIES and
other ways

God
Speaks
to
Guys

Randall Cirner

SERVANT
BOOKS

PUBLISHED BY ST. ANTHONY MESSENGER PRESS
CINCINNATI, OHIO

Cover design by Dave Hile
Book design by Emily Schneider

Library of Congress Cataloging-in-Publication Data

Cirner, Randall.
  White water, bears, dry flies, and other ways God speaks to guys / by Randall Cirner.
      p. cm.
   ISBN 0-86716-618-5 (alk. paper)
   1. Christian men—Religious life. 2. Christian life—Meditations. I. Title.

BV4528.2.C57 2004
242'.642—dc22

                                        2004015666

ISBN 0-86716-618-5

Published by Servant Books, an imprint of St. Anthony Messenger Press
www.AmericanCatholic.org

Printed in the United States of America.

Table of Contents

Acknowledgments

To Therese, my wife and friend for thirty-five years,
thanks for your constant encouragement.

To Jenni, Tom, Cathy, Reeb, Steven, and, of course, Tim.

Note to the Reader

As you will see in these pages, I'm one of those people who see and make connections—parallels—between what is happening in my life and what God says to us in Scripture. The following personal stories and the meditations that accompany them are meant to illustrate how God teaches us through many means—not the least of which is the "stuff" of daily life. My lessons were learned, for the most part, when I was engaged in some outdoor activity—downhill skiing, hiking, fishing, hunting, gardening, pruning. I find God readily in the beauty of his creation and through my attempts to enjoy it. I hope you find both enjoyment and inspiration from this book.

May God bless you as you apply the lessons I've learned and also as you have opportunity to see spiritual parallels in your backyard.

1

Faster Isn't Always Better

I was out of control, careening straight down the hill, skis flat, poles useless, praying fervently that I wouldn't hit any other skiers. Having never experienced this lack of control, I was terrified.

I was on an expert slope at Boyne Mountain, Michigan. I had learned to ski a few years earlier and was better than a novice but not firmly an intermediate downhill skier. Earlier that day I had felt pretty confident on the intermediate slopes.

Then, convinced that to be an expert skier one had to ski the expert slopes, I took the lift to the top of one. Looking down, I saw that the angle of descent was much steeper than it had appeared at the bottom. My confidence ebbed a mite, but no good skier turns away from such a challenge (not to mention that there was no way off the mountain except down the slope). So off I went, carving easy S-curves with my ski edges. As my speed increased, I lost my rhythm. The next thing I knew, I was out of control, hurtling down the slope faster than I ever thought possible. Panicked, I knew the only way out of this was a bailout. Taking one more fearful gulp of air, I hit the ground. My skis and poles went flying as I slid down the mountain in a cloud of snow and ice, winding up in a bedraggled heap at the bottom. What a run!

Lying there I remembered the old adage that faster is not necessarily better. I went back to the intermediate slopes.

■

As a skier, I tried to leapfrog from novice-intermediate to expert in one quick slope. We face a similar temptation when it comes to the spiritual life. We want to make progress in our Christian growth, becoming holy, prayerful, humble, and loving. We look around and see that others seem to be more advanced in the spiritual life than we are. Some people, for example, may have a daily personal prayer time; they go to Mass every day and pray the rosary regularly. They seem able to understand and love people with great ease and facility. They spend time in service to others.

When we compare ourselves with such people, it's easy to feel spiritually inadequate. So in response we do more "expert" things to help us grow faster spiritually. The problem, of course, is that we can't leapfrog into a more expert status in the spiritual life any more than I could leapfrog into expert status in downhill skiing. If we attempt a super-fast method of growth, we will eventually crash. Trying to do things we are not ready for, even if we seem to handle it at the beginning, eventually leads to a bailout.

It is not easy to recover from a spiritual bailout. We are inclined not to go back to a moderate level but rather to regress to a more primitive stage of our spiritual life. This is a normal reaction to the intensity of what we attempted and failed.

Our life in the Lord is a natural growth process. Each of us needs to proceed at an individual pace. There is no secret formula for rapid growth. There is no spiritual Miracle-Gro. The Lord works his grace within each of us in his right time to bring us closer to him, to root out sin, and to help us grow in virtue.

Now, as you begin this book of reflections, is a good time to evaluate your spiritual life and to set goals for growth. But be careful not to bite off more than you can chew. Think in terms of patience, balance, and trust.

God will achieve all that he intends for us. He does not ask us to be on the fast track but to be faithful to where we are at this moment.

For Personal Reflection and Response
When did you last review your spiritual life? Are you trying to do too much? Are you satisfied with too little? Consider setting aside time each day for prayer, Scripture reading, talking to God. In a month or so, review how things are going and make some adjustments.

Scripture for Meditation
For everything there is a season, and a time for every matter under heaven.

ECCLESIASTES 3:1

2

Get That First Nail Centered

I come from a line of carpenters. My father's father was a carpenter in Slovakia before immigrating to the United States. He then worked as a carpenter in various cities in the Midwest before settling in a small town in Michigan. My father also worked with wood most of his life and was an excellent carpenter in his own right. I inherited their love for woodworking and have completed various projects over the years.

When I was seven years old, my father helped our neighbor across the street build a new house. I had my own carpenter apron and hammer, which my dad had given me one Christmas. I begged him to allow me to help. He looked doubtful but agreed. With great excitement, I went to my first carpentry job the following Saturday.

The owner gave me a handful of nails and told me to fasten one section of the subfloor to the floor joist. He emphasized that I needed to keep an eye on where my previous nails were to make sure that I was going in a straight line. This ensured that each nail was going into the joist. By the time I finished, I had the straightest line of nails I had ever seen. When the owner came over to inspect my work, I saw a puzzled look on his face. He disappeared for a couple of minutes. When he returned he asked me to look at something with him.

He took me into the basement so that we were standing directly under the area where I had fastened my nails. There it was—twenty feet of nails in a perfectly straight line, every nail missing the floor joist by exactly three inches. I had aligned the nails perfectly. The problem was that I had started three inches off the mark. I learned an important carpentry lesson that day: As important as it is to have all your nails in a straight row, it is even more important that the first nail be on target.

■

The cornerstone of our Christian faith is that God loves us unconditionally. He has shown that love by sending his Son to suffer and die for us. It is critical that we get this "nail" properly positioned so that the rest of our Christian life can line up. It often happens, however, that this nail is misaligned just slightly and misses the "unconditional" joist. Many sincere Christians believe that God loves them only when they do good things. If we think this way, we focus on performance, trying to look good for God. Our life may seem perfect to other people, but we have actually missed the point. Performance-oriented Christians can be in the grip of fear, scrupulosity, or religious compulsion, because they sense that God's love and favor are dependent upon externals. Such an approach to Christian faith is based upon a false assumption.

God's love is not at all like human love that often fluctuates depending on how things are going in a relationship. If we could only understand the magnitude of the Father's gift to us in Jesus and the tremendous love shown in Christ's death and resurrection, we would get the nail of Christ's love firmly in the right place. Jesus, stretched out on the cross, is the Father's eternal sign of his incomprehensible and complete love for us. Nothing can get in the way of that love. Our sin can cut us off from experiencing that love, but even sin does not cut us off from the fact of God's love.

If we live in the assurance of God's unconditional love for us, we are able to love others unconditionally. If that nail is lined up right, everything else in life will follow. We live according to God's laws because we know God loves us and we want to please him, not because we are afraid of losing his love if we don't.

For Personal Reflection and Response
The truth in Scripture has great power to help us change. As you meditate on the passages below, ask God to help you release your fears and doubts about his love for you and accept the truth proclaimed in his Word.

Scripture for Meditation
In this is love, not that we loved God but that he loved us and sent his Son to be the atoning sacrifice for our sins.

1 JOHN 4:10

For I am convinced that neither death, nor life, nor angels, nor rulers, nor things present, nor things to come, nor powers, nor height, nor depth, nor anything else in all creation, will be able to separate us from the love of God in Christ Jesus our Lord.

ROMANS 8:38-39

3

You Don't Need All That Stuff

My feet were blistered, my shoulders ached from the backpack, and I had a rope burn across my neck from carrying a poorly positioned sleeping bag. A group of us, all in our mid-twenties, were hiking to the top of one of the higher peaks in the Great Smoky Mountains National Park. We planned to spend the night at one of the partial shelters that dot the Appalachian Trail.

We were walking behind a group of hikers who carried only water bottles and hiking staffs. With this group was a girl about twelve years old, who kept bounding up ahead of her group and running back down to meet them. She seemed to have limitless energy. About three-quarters of the way up the mountain, when our group was really dragging, she returned from one of her forward expeditions with the joyful exclamation, "They're having Salisbury steak at the lodge tonight."

I thought, Salisbury steak at the lodge tonight?! So that was why they needed only water bottles and no other camping equipment. Food and lodging were provided.

■

The contrast between the two hiking groups was striking. Our group was bent over with heavy backpacks carrying food, sleeping bags, cooking equipment, all those things we needed to spend a night in an open shelter on top of the mountain. We staggered up the mountain. Because of our age, we put the best face on it and acted as if we climbed such peaks every day. In truth we were all tired and exhausted, but nobody would admit it. The other group, carrying only water bottles, was enjoying a moderately difficult walk. (Even without equipment, you can't climb three thousand feet and not be affected by it.)

It irritated me to realize that people could climb this mountain and find a hotel at the top of it. I had thought this was a peak climbed only by the hale and hearty, those willing to rough it and spend a cold night outside.

How many of us walk up "the mountain of the Lord" burdened down by all kinds of baggage? We insist on carrying equipment with the mistaken notion that we are going to "need this" somewhere along the line. For example, how many of us unnecessarily carry an "image" we project to those around us, because we want to be considered a particular type of person? Maybe we want to pro-ject a macho image, impervious to pain or difficulty; or perhaps a very pious image, busy with prayers, sacrifices, and other spiritual activities. Still others project an image of being "real people," partying and drinking, not like those holy rollers. Each of these images can become a burden of our own making.

We also become burdened by our sins. Sin can bring us some fleeting pleasure, but in the end it causes us more harm than good. We like to indulge ourselves a little, yet the more we hang on to sins, the heavier they get as we approach the top of the mountain.

Don't we all long to be like the young girl, unencumbered by burdens and able to skip up and down the mountain? She knew that there was a lodge at the top of the mountain, where she could find shelter and enjoy a great meal. She was unconcerned about carrying unnecessary things with her.

Do you believe that the kind of lodging and food that awaits you at the end of your journey is substantial enough that you don't have to bring other equipment along? What "stuff" are you unnecessarily carrying? Why not begin now to unshoulder some of these burdens? Take the risk. Shed that image that you try to project to others. Let go of self-concern. God never intended us to carry these things. Let Jesus free the burden from your shoulder. Let's skip up his mountain with joy in our hearts, a lightness on our backs, and a song on our lips.

For Personal Reflection and Response
Imagine that you are carrying a heavy pack loaded with your "stuff." Examine each item and prayerfully consider whether or not you really need it for your journey.

Scripture for Meditation
I relieved your shoulder of the burden;
    your hands were freed from the basket.

PSALM 81:6

4

Keep Your Eyes on the Horizon

It was 5:30 A.M. On a small fishing boat we were headed to a reef twenty-five miles into the Atlantic to fish for shark. It was a beautiful day. The sunrise over the water was absolutely gorgeous, and the weather report for the day was fantastic: clear skies and temperature in the low eighties. I was excited and exhilarated with anticipation.

But after an hour or two, my head hurt and my stomach felt queasy. Some of my friends were feeling worse than I. They had to go below, lie down, and eat saltines to settle their stomachs. We were seasick. When the captain of the boat saw how we were feeling, he said, "Keep your eyes on the horizon. Look far ahead, and you will feel better." I took his advice, forcing my eyes toward the horizon rather than looking at the closer swells. Gradually, my seasickness subsided. My friends, however, were not able to keep focused, and they spent the rest of the trip feeling miserable.

■

I later learned that keeping the eyes focused on the horizon flattens the visual cues caused by sea swells. The eye then sends a message to the inner ear, which regains a sense of equilibrium. This stops the physical reaction—seasickness—to the sense of motion.

Life is often compared to a ship at sea. When life gets rough and our personal seas get stormy, it's easy to lose perspective and become focused on our immediate circumstances. We may fall upon hard financial times or have a relationship go bad. Or God may seem far away, as if he's not answering our prayers. During such times we are tempted to focus on the immediate. We are misled into thinking that what is happening right now will last for the rest of our lives, that things will only go from bad to worse. We have taken our eyes off the horizon, the Lord, and have focused on the immediate waves.

At other times the seas are calm. We seem to ride evenly upon the gentle swells of life. But even at these times we can lose perspective, not because things are going badly, but precisely because things are going well. We can mistakenly think the good things are due to our own efforts or initiatives. As we focus on our immediate good circumstances, we also take our eyes off the spiritual horizon, the Lord. In these times it's not so much that we sink into desperation or hopelessness but into complacency. We focus on the material aspects and lose sight of the true spiritual reality behind it all. How often do we find our prayer lives beginning to slip during times of ease and comfort? When we become content with immediate good things and lose sight of growth in intimacy with the Lord, we lose perspective and become seasick. The complacency of materialism, the lulling effect of the world, the deadening effects of engaging in sensual pleasures can make us spiritually seasick at a time when we think things are relatively calm.

The challenge for us as Christians is to keep our eyes always on the Lord and to not lose sight of him in either good times or bad times. If we keep our eyes on the horizon, we will be able to navigate through any waters.

For Personal Reflection and Response

What are some of the concerns that keep you from being focused on Jesus—the horizon? Pray the following focus prayer as often as necessary to keep your eyes on Jesus:

Lord Jesus, you are my spiritual horizon. I desire to keep my eyes on you today. I place in your hands my concerns and ask that you take care of them. May the Holy Spirit increase my trust as I focus on you. Amen.

Scripture for Meditation

Immediately [Jesus] made the disciples get into the boat and go on ahead to the other side, while he dismissed the crowds. And after he had dismissed the crowds, he went up the mountain by himself to pray. When evening came, he was there alone, but by this time the boat, battered by the waves, was far from the land, for the wind was against them. And early in the morning he came walking toward them on the sea. But when the disciples saw him walking on the sea, they were terrified, saying, "It is a ghost!" And they cried out in fear. But immediately Jesus spoke to them and said, "Take heart, it is I; do not be afraid."

Peter answered him, "Lord, if it is you, command me to come to you on the water." He said, "Come." So Peter got out of the boat, started walking on the water, and came toward Jesus. But when he noticed the strong wind, he became frightened, and beginning to sink, he cried out, "Lord, save me!" Jesus immediately reached out his hand and caught him, saying to him, "You of little faith, why did you doubt?" When they got into the boat, the wind ceased.

MATTHEW 14:22-32

5

For God So Loved the World

On a recent trip to Austria I hiked in a nature park, where I was immensely impressed by the awesome beauty that surrounded me. As I walked along the path, the river running full torrent at my feet, I could look up and see sheer rock cliffs on either side of me rising hundreds of feet. The forest floor was bursting with various colored wildflowers. Perhaps the most awesome spectacle was the number of waterfalls cascading down the face of the cliffs. The waterfalls and the river caused a constant muffled roar along the entire path.

At times like these I become painfully aware of how insignificant my life seems in the face of the awesome majesty and beauty of God's creation. Walking that path I was conscious that the river and waterfalls had been here for thousands, if not millions, of years and that the towering cliffs had been formed by the river. The river, the cliffs, the waterfalls, and the forest had been here ages before I was born and would continue long after I departed. Something of the infinite in the scene around me made me feel very small.

■

At times we all feel relatively unimportant when we consider the cosmic scheme of things. We seem to be a mere speck of dust on an infinite plane. We are tempted to think that God does not know who we are or remember that we are here. If misfortune strikes or we are down emotionally or dry spiritually, it can seem as though we are alone and forgotten in the world. If our friends slight us, we may take it so seriously that we withdraw and experience that awful sense of aloneness. It is sometimes hard to believe that we are loved and lovable. *Does anyone really care about me?* we wonder.

But consider the incredible love that God has shown us in Christ. Christ was born for each one of us individually, as a unique person. As much as I was awestruck by the beauty of the Austrian mountains, rivers, waterfalls, and wildflowers, Christ didn't come for mountains, hills, waterfalls, and wildflowers. Christ came for human beings. Christ was born for me and for you. This is something that raises us to a stature far above any other created things. Even in our most serious loneliness or sinful disfiguration, we are still loved by the Lord. We are of infinitely more worth to him than anything else he created.

Let's not lose sight of the fact that Christ's birth was a personal act of love for each of us. Although we may believe that we are small and insignificant, God's love raises us to a new significance. He invites us to a profound level of friendship and relationship with him.

Yes, in many respects, we are small in relation to the created nature of things. But when Christ became human, he raised us to a whole new level of existence. To paraphrase C. S. Lewis, in *Prince Caspian,* one of the *Chronicles of Narnia:* Being a son of Adam or a daughter of Eve should raise the head of the lowliest beggar and bow the head of the greatest king.

For Personal Reflection and Response

Look for an opportunity to spend a few minutes looking at a manger scene in an art book or museum, in a church, on a Christmas card you've stored away. Or take special note of a baby you see, in a store or park or at church. Allow the manger scene or the baby to represent God incarnate, and in so doing ask the Spirit to help you understand God's personal love for you.

Scripture for Meditation

When I look at your heavens, the work of your fingers,
  the moon and the stars that you have established;
what are human beings that you are mindful of them,
  mortals that you care for them?

Yet you have made them a little lower than God,
  and crowned them with glory and honor.

PSALM 8:3-5

6
The Ready Position

I was in sixth grade and wanted to be a football player like the big guys at school. This was my chance to make the team, but I was not making a very good showing of it. I stood there feeling stupid and incompetent. I hadn't made a tackle all afternoon. Ball carriers ran past me on the right, then on the left, then right over the top of me. By the time I reacted to the flow of a play, it was too late. The coaches paid more attention to the running backs and didn't particularly care that I wasn't making any tackles.

Finally, one of the coaches came over to me and said, "You're standing flat footed. You are not ready for what may come your direction." He then explained what he called the "ready position." He showed me how to flex slightly at the knees, resting lightly on the balls of my feet, weight forward, hands out rather than at my side, head up. He said this was the basic athletic position needed for every sport. Standing in this position enabled a player to react quickly and move in any direction with agility. Standing flat footed, weight back on my heels, arms at my side, the way I had been, was an invitation to be beaten every time.

With patience and practice I was able to master the ready position, and I eventually became a passably decent linebacker for our football team.

■

The lesson about the ready position has stayed with me my entire life. The coach was absolutely right. Whether I was playing football, baseball, tennis, volleyball—no matter what the sport—the ready position was the fundamental position necessary to play the game successfully.

As Christians we have a ready position that enables us to respond to the movements of the Holy Spirit. That position is on our knees in prayer. Prayer puts us in touch with God in a way that nothing else can. In prayer we can hear what God may be speaking to us; we can perceive what he is presently doing in our lives, and we can respond to him. Being in the ready position of prayer enables us to move in the same direction as the Lord.

Let's take the time to learn or improve this basic position. Learning the prayer ready position takes practice, just as it does with learning the athletic ready position. We have to practice it every day until it becomes second nature. After the coach showed me the ready position in football and I practiced it regularly, it became such a natural stance that it would never have entered my mind to stand in any other position on the field. Having learned the lesson for the football field, it was easy for me to carry it over to all the other sports I played. It became a natural part of my life.

The Lord wants prayer to be a natural part of our lives. He wants us to feel normal and natural about being in this position no matter where we are. That is why he wants us to practice the habit of prayer every day. Personal prayer brings us closer to the Lord and enables us to have our minds and hearts focused on that which is most important, life in Christ. Prayer helps us keep perspective and strengthens and renews us every day, as we become more and more intimate with the Lord Jesus Christ.

Some may feel comfortable praying in a familiar place, such as church, but may feel less comfortable praying in other places, such as while driving the car, walking across town, or running around a track. The point of practicing prayer and learning the ready position is that we become more familiar with it and then are able to do it naturally in a wider variety of places.

Busyness, distraction, forgetfulness, or fatigue can keep us from daily personal prayer. So it may be a good idea to schedule a specific time for prayer each day. Many people find it most helpful to pray first thing in the morning before the distractions of the day begin. The important thing, however, is to start with a manageable amount of time and be persistent about it. No matter how uncomfortable it may seem at first, with persistence prayer will eventually become a natural part of life.

For Personal Reflection and Response
Do you have a habit of daily prayer? If not, start with just a few minutes and then gradually increase them until you find the amount of time that is right for you. The important thing is to be faithful to prayer every day. There are many forms of prayer (such as the Lord's Prayer, those found in prayer books, the rosary, psalms, spontaneous prayer). You can experiment and find the forms most comfortable for you.

Scripture for Meditation
Devote yourselves to prayer, keeping alert in it with thanksgiving.

COLOSSIANS 4:2

Do not worry about anything, but in everything by prayer and supplication with thanksgiving let your requests be made known to God. And the peace of God, which surpasses all understanding, will guard your hearts and your minds in Christ Jesus.

PHILIPPIANS 4:6-7

7

A Time for Refreshment

I looked around the barn in amazement. There were clothes and personal items strewn everywhere. I ran out of the barn and burst into the house, "Grandpa, Grandpa!" I said, "There are clothes and things all over the barn. Are there robbers around?"

"It's all right," he said, "I let people change in the barn so they can swim in the lake." He explained that the clothes belonged to seasonal workers harvesting one of the crops around Hart, Michigan. "Those folks work hard," he said, "and they need time to recuperate." I knew what he meant. I had helped him pick apples and peaches in his orchards, and it was hot, tiring work.

∎

I was impressed with my grandfather's concern for these strangers. The life of a seasonal worker is not easy. It's hot, hard, dusty work. The workers move from place to place, living from hand to mouth, with few long-term relationships to count on. My grandfather gave them an opportunity to stop for a while and get refreshed. He allowed them to forget about the next bushel of peaches to be picked and to focus on fun with their families.

We all need refreshment. The work we do is hard, whether we are students, laborers, officer workers, professionals, or caring for families. We get tired; we get hot; we can lose our perspective. The daily grind takes its toll on us. Even though we are doing it for God and are trying to live in the power of the Holy Spirit, we still get tired.

Our minds, bodies, and spirits are still subject to the cares, worries, and weight of our daily lives. We need some time to ease back.

I'm writing this chapter during Lent. Most of us tend to think of Lent as a time of spiritual and physical rigors that are supposed to be more draining and difficult than usual. But in fact, our additional disciplines are meant to bring us spiritual refreshment. Lent is the church's retreat, a time when the church steps aside from the daily routines and cares of life and invites us to focus on Christ and grow in a relationship with him. Our Lenten retreat affords us time to take our eyes off the present and look to the future. Where are we going, why are we going there, and what will enable us to achieve our goals?

No matter what the season of the year, ask yourself: What type of refreshment do I need? What burdens are weighing me down right now? What challenges am I facing in my walk with Christ? Let's step back and take a serious look at these areas, through prayer, Scripture reading, and fasting. The cooling water of the Holy Spirit will bathe us in refreshment and renewal as we open ourselves to his action. Let's give him free rein to refocus or adjust our goals or activities to enable us to grow closer to Christ. If we take this approach, our vision and focus for life will be sharpened; we will return to daily life with a renewed sense of purpose and mission, empowered by the Holy Spirit for what he calls us to do.

For Personal Reflection and Response

What spiritual struggles are you experiencing right now? Try putting them aside and do something you find refreshing (for example, read the life of a saint or a spiritual person you admire; read your favorite Bible stories or passages; listen to spiritually uplifting music).

Scripture for Meditation
He said to them, "Come away to a deserted place all by yourselves and rest a while."

MARK 6:31

8

Blessed Are the Poor in Spirit

We were ready. Pots of spaghetti sat on the serving table along with bread, vegetables, and dessert. All of the tables were set with the proper utensils. All we needed was our first "customer." Nobody showed up. We grew a little anxious. Finally, twenty minutes after we were supposed to begin serving dinner, the first person arrived. He came in the door, looked shyly around, and asked, "Is this the place where we eat dinner?"

"Sure," one of us replied, "come on in."

Eventually other people drifted in by twos and threes, until nearly thirty people were eating the spaghetti dinner we had prepared.

These were homeless people. During the week, area churches took turns providing meals for the homeless and serving them at this particular homeless shelter. But on weekends no church was able to serve meals. When our Christian community in Ann Arbor discovered this, some of us decided to serve a Saturday dinner.

■

We were all apprehensive when we began this project. This was a new world for most of us middle-class folk. I had never been homeless, never had to miss more than one or two meals, always had clothes to wear. I could walk into any store or place of business in the city and be treated with respect. Now married, with children, I saw homeless people only from a distance as I drove down the street. I had never been to a homeless shelter.

Over the weeks, months, and years that we prepared and served this meal, we learned a lot of things. Some of the homeless were polite, some were rude; some looked you in the eye, some never raised their eyes from the floor; some were talkative, others taciturn; some were perpetually happy, others seemed always burdened; some would let you into their lives, some would not; some had positive hopes and dreams for the future, others felt very hopeless. The church asks all Catholics to take a special concern for the homeless. We should take both a material and spiritual concern for people throughout the world, but especially for those in our own cities and neighborhoods who, for one reason or another, have no place to live.

We aren't always aware of the needs of the people in our area. We don't often see the homeless or the hungry or those in need of clothing. Certainly some of us don't have much money or a wide variety of clothes in our closets, but that is not the same as the plight of the homeless.

It takes an effort to break out of our comfortable lives and mix with those who are poor. From a spiritual point of view, all of us should see ourselves as homeless and poor. The New Testament teaches us to recognize that this current life and world are not our true home. We are wanderers, looking for and hoping for the home of heaven that awaits us. We are pilgrims, not looking to settle in here. The New Testament teaches us to be poor in spirit, to shed the accretions of materialism and consumerism that are so much a part of our society. We are to be detached from things so that we can be perfectly happy whether we find ourselves in plenty or in want.

Let's become rich by sharing in others' poverty; be more fully clothed by sharing our clothing with those who are naked; become more sure of our own dwelling by taking care of those who currently have no place to live.

For Personal Reflection and Response
What is your attitude toward the poor and homeless? What personal obstacles do you need to overcome to serve them? Consider volunteering at a shelter or soup kitchen. If you do, you may be surprised at how your attitude toward the poor changes.

Scripture for Meditation
Truly I tell you, just as you did it to one of the least of these who are members of my family, you did it to me.

MATTHEW 25:40

9

The Perfect Tree

"Hey Dad," my daughter said, "Here's a nice tree. How about this one?" I held the evergreen upright, turned it around, looking at all sides, and said, "No, this won't do. There aren't enough branches." We continued looking through the Christmas tree lot. My daughter called out from another section, "Hey Dad, how about this one?" I looked it over. "Nope," I said, "it has two trunks."

We moved on through the lot. Each time my daughter found a tree, I rejected it. My daughter was used to this. Each year we go through the same routine. But finally, after stopping at a number of tree lots, we finally found one that satisfied her specifications and mine.

■

We all have an image of what makes a beautiful Christmas tree. Most of us want a tree that tapers at the top, where we can place a star or an angel. We like it to be cone shaped with enough branches to give it a "full" look. When I was a child, I thought that Christmas trees grew in that cone-shaped fashion. I don't know when I first discovered that they didn't, but during my high school and college years I found out how it works. I had summer jobs on large tree farms, where I pruned pine trees with a sharp machete so they would look like our image of Christmas trees. I learned how to work with a tree to help its natural growth conform to a cone-shaped pattern. I learned how to trim off the top whorl of a tree so one branch was dominant; how to cut out a double-trunk tree so it had a single trunk growing straight; how to shape the tree from the top out. Sometimes the trimming was minor, sometimes major.

In the spiritual life we want to conform our lives to Jesus. But just as Christmas trees don't grow naturally in a cone shape, neither do we grow naturally in a Christ shape. For us to take on the likeness of Christ, we need to have work done to us. The Holy Spirit is a master tree shaper. He knows what needs to be done so we can be shaped into the likeness of Christ. Things can get painful as the Holy Spirit cuts back something we thought looked pretty. Sometimes he works on us because we have two trunks; we are double minded. We want to be like Christ, but we also want to be like the world. Every tree farmer knows a good tree cannot have two trunks; one has to be cut out.

If we want to be conformed to the image of Christ, we have to be put under his shaping knife. Catherine of Siena, Mother Teresa, Francis of Assisi, Ignatius of Loyola, all had to undergo this shaping. The more perfectly you want to be conformed to Christ, the more you need to submit to radical shaping.

This shaping is not a one-time deal. Evergreens that are going to become Christmas trees need to be trimmed every summer until they are cut and sent to a tree lot. This is because they put on new growth, which needs to be formed. As we continue to grow, we take on things that are not in conformity with Christ. Our human nature puts on growth, such as pride, self-concern, greed, and sinful habits or inclinations. Envy, foul language, judgmentalism, bigotry, and lying sprout new branches. Consequently we will always "be under the knife" as the Holy Spirit works to shape us into the image of Christ. We endure this work of the Holy Spirit, because we hope one day to hear the words of Jesus, "Take this one, Father, because it is perfectly shaped."

For Personal Reflection and Response
In what ways is God shaping your life at the present time? As you reflect on his sometimes painful trimming, try to keep in mind his ultimate goal and thank him for his love.

Scripture for Meditation
Even though our outer nature is wasting away, our inner nature is being renewed day by day.

2 CORINTHIANS 4:16

10

Eight-Year-Olds Become Nine-Year-Olds

The baseball made a high arc in the sky and started its descent, toward me. I put up my glove and ran to the spot where I expected it to come down. It fell behind me. The coach who had thrown the ball had already picked up a second one. The second ball was in the air. Again I put up my glove and ran toward it. This one fell at my side. The third ball came. Glove in the air, eyes wide, concentrating, I was right under it. It hit me on top of the head and bounced away.

I was eight years old, trying out for Little League. The coaches gave each of us an opportunity to catch a few balls to check our eye-hand coordination and reflexes. Feeling dejected, I stood with my dad on the sidelines and watched the other eight-year-olds perform. They all fared pretty much like me. In the end none of us made a team. On the ride home my dad said to me, "Don't feel too bad. Your eye-hand coordination will improve, and, if you keep practicing, you will make the team next year." He was right.

The following year I was amazed at how much easier it was to catch the ball, at the effortless way the glove came to the spot where the ball was going to be, at the way my eye followed the ball into the glove and the natural way my hand closed when the ball hit the pocket of the glove. The difference one year made in my ability to catch a fly ball was striking. Much of the change was due to natural growth and development. My eye-hand coordination improved because I had grown older. I had continued to play baseball and practice my technique, but the major factor was my advanced developmental capability. At nine, I was ready to catch a baseball.

■

Some of us, in our zeal, assume that we are capable of great acts of spiritual discipline. We want to be like the people around us who, especially during Lent, take on more prayer, fasting, almsgiving, and works of mercy. But when this spiritual ball gets up in the air, we are just not able to handle it. We get discouraged and think we are not as spiritual as we should be. We forget that the spiritual life has a developmental nature to it.

Young Christians don't always possess the spiritual eye-hand coordination that enables them to handle high-flying spiritual activities. As an eight-year-old I was able to catch balls that my dad threw to me in the backyard. That was because my dad was throwing from just a few feet away and not throwing the ball too high or too hard. This gave me an opportunity to develop both my eye-hand coordination and my confidence. But the high, hard ones being thrown at Little League tryouts eluded me.

Each person needs to understand his or her own spiritual development in order to adequately assess the kinds of spiritual activities to undertake. Looking around at other people and trying to gauge what I ought to be doing on the basis of what other people seem to be doing is a sure road to discouragement. Christ invites each one of us to do those things that will allow us to grow closer to him. He doesn't ask us all to do the same things with the same vigor. Before you decide you are going to go after the "high, hard ones," take stock of your own spiritual development. Check with your confessor before you decide to take on disciplines that may stretch you beyond where you ought to go at this point.

Certainly the other side of the coin is that we can be too easy on ourselves. We don't like pain, we don't like to feel uncomfortable, so we don't move into another zone where we can grow. Feeling stretched in our spiritual life is not always a sign of biting off more than we can chew.

What we need is wise self-understanding and insight into our spiritual development. Know yourself. Be generous toward God. Set your sights realistically.

For Personal Reflection and Response
Think of times in your life when you suddenly found that you could do something you couldn't do before (for example, ride a bike, roller-skate, hit a ball). What made the difference? How much was due to practice? How much was due to being older and more mature?

In your current relationship with God, what *one* thing would you like to change? How do you think it can change?

Scripture for Meditation
Be imitators of God, as beloved children, and live in love, as Christ loved us and gave himself up for us.

EPHESIANS 5:1

11

At Your Service

A few months after we had begun serving a weekly meal to the homeless, one of the crews returned from its rotation and declared that it wasn't sure it wanted to continue. The clients seemed rather ungrateful about the whole thing. We all knew what this crew was saying. Seldom did anyone say thank you for the meal served. Most acted as if the meal was a right.

When the homeless people became sure that we were going to be back every Saturday, they awaited our arrival and greeted us with impatience. If we were a little late, some were upset.

If the food was not up to someone's expectation, we heard about it. If the food ran short due to an unexpectedly large turnout, we heard about it. It was beginning to bother most of us.

We had a long talk that evening about what our attitude needed to be. We all had an expectation that homeless people ought to be very grateful for what we were doing. After all, we had given up a Saturday afternoon and part of the evening to prepare and serve a meal and clean up afterward. We were so taken with our magnanimous gesture of self-giving that we thought everybody would see it as we did. It was a shock to discover that not everyone did. We were disappointed. We were hurt. Lack of recognition and gratitude had dulled our commitment. Our focus had shifted from serving the Lord and his "little ones" and fastened on ourselves as wonderful people to be doing such a noble task.

■

Jesus never said that we should expect gratitude for the service we perform on his behalf. In fact, Jesus had some of his harshest criticism for the Pharisees who did things in order to be seen and praised by others. The Gospel of Luke tells us that when we have finished all of our hard work for the Lord, our response should be, "We are unworthy servants or worthless slaves. We have done only what we ought to have done." This is a noble ideal that I find easier to maintain in the abstract than the concrete.

Don't we all? Do we find ourselves doing things mainly for people who notice and express gratitude? Aren't we more willing to do that little extra to clean the room if we know someone will notice? But what about the people who never acknowledge what we do for them?

Our service to Christ in others—whether they are homeless, a roommate, a family member, or a coworker—is its own reward. It is a privilege to serve Christ. Let's take time to grow in the virtue of selfless service. Look for opportunities to do things for those who cannot repay you or who might not notice. Remember Christ on the cross. It is an excellent reminder that we can never hope to repay what he did for us. It is also an opportunity to meditate on how ungrateful we can be for Christ's tremendous sacrifice.

For Personal Reflection and Response

As you consider Christ's sacrifice of himself for you, try to identify your feelings. Do you feel grateful, neutral, indifferent, (something else) about his sacrifice?

Name any people who irritate you because they don't acknowledge you when you do something for them. What needs to change so that you can serve them without looking for thanks?

Scripture for Meditation

So you also, when you have done all that you were ordered to do, say, "We are worthless slaves; we have done only what we ought to have done!"

LUKE 17:10

12

Watch Out for Those Spiritual Hot Spots!

My feet were on fire. I dropped my backpack along the side of the trail and sat down on the ground. Taking off my boots, I examined my feet and realized I was in serious trouble. I had gone less than halfway to my intended destination along the Appalachian Trail that day. From the condition of my feet, I knew I couldn't go on. I would have to spend the night right there. It was not a particularly good site, but I had no other choice. As I hobbled around my little camp that night, I had some choice words for my own stupidity at not taking proper care of my feet.

Before I left my car that morning, something had nudged me to put additional protection on my feet, because I hadn't worn my hiking boots for some time. But I had decided not to take the time to do so, and off I had gone, with a sixty-five-pound pack on my back. I wasn't long on the trail before I developed hot spots on my heels. That should have been a warning to me. But I had ignored them and pushed on. A little while later the hot spots had disappeared, replaced by that telltale bump signaling a blister. Again, I had known I should stop and do something, but I hadn't. Eventually the blisters broke, and I was left with raw flesh chafing against my boots with every step.

Examining my feet the next morning, I knew I was finished. My hope of having four days on the Appalachian Trail by myself had come to an end. I put some dressing on my feet, lightened my pack as best as I could, and hobbled back down the trail to my car. I drove home with bare feet. I couldn't wear shoes for the next three days.

■

On our journey through life there are things we know we need to take care of, but we don't. This can lead to serious trouble for us down the road. For example, Scripture teaches us that forgiveness is an important aspect of the

Christian life. Periodically people do things that injure us. Our friends, our parents, our children, our brothers and sisters let us down or hurt us in both small and major ways.

If we don't take care of these hurts through forgiveness, they become like heels rubbing against boots. First they turn into spiritual hot spots. Hot spots lead to blisters, and blisters, if they are not taken care of, break and leave raw nerves exposed to increasing irritation. Lack of forgiveness operates like a constant friction that chafes against our spirits. Unforgiven hurts can become open wounds that are not just incredibly painful, but can also be crippling. I know people who became bitter and resentful because they had been unable to forgive an injury done to them years ago. Their lives are now ruled by a bitterness that started with a single unwillingness to forgive.

Forgiving hurts, especially major ones, is not something we can do on our own. The power to forgive isn't merely a human action, but a divine action as well. We need the grace of God to offer deep, sincere forgiveness to people who have hurt us. It's only as we live in the heart of Christ that we are able to leave behind our own pain and hurt, freeing ourselves from the bondage of resentment and bitterness. Forgiveness removes the focus from our own pain. Forgiveness is great freedom. Forgiveness is like plunging our blistered feet into a cool mountain stream. It sends refreshment not just to our feet, but also through our whole bodies.

Look at how God in Christ forgave us, and follow his example. We can free ourselves from the agony of injuries that are unforgiven by dealing with spiritual hot spots immediately. Let's not allow them to become raw, open wounds. Our walk along the trail of life will be more enjoyable and much less painful.

For Personal Reflection and Response

If you feel ready to let go of some of the hurts in your life, I recommend this method: After prayerful consideration, take separate slips of paper and on each sheet, write one hurt you have a hard time forgiving. Get a medium-sized crucifix and "nail" (tape) each hurt to the cross. As you put each hurt on the cross, say, "Lord Jesus, as you forgive me, so I forgive *(name)* for *(name the offense)*. I now leave it on your cross and ask you to give me the grace to live in freedom from anger, bitterness, and resentment."

If there is a hurt you have a very hard time forgiving, consider bringing it to the sacrament of reconciliation and discuss it with a confessor.

Scripture for Meditation

Bear with the other and, if anyone has a complaint against another, forgive each other; just as the Lord has forgiven you, so you also must forgive.

COLOSSIANS 3:13

13

What Will Be Left for Me?

Some years ago one of my brothers and one of my sisters were both diagnosed as having a degenerative kidney disease. There was no telling how quickly the disease would progress. Eventually my brother's kidneys failed completely, and he was on dialysis three days a week. There were only two real options for him: He could remain on dialysis for the rest of his life, which meant he could never be far from a dialysis machine. Or he could receive a kidney transplant. He tried dialysis for some time but finally had to admit he needed a transplant.

The best donors for kidneys are other family members. This meant that my other healthy brother and I were prime candidates to donate a kidney.

As we began the screening process, I realized I knew very little about the procedure. I didn't know how the donation surgery would affect my own life. Yes, I was aware that a person could live with only one functioning kidney, but I had no idea what "to live" meant. I feared that it meant a lifestyle of less strenuous activity, restricted diet, and frequent medical checkups.

An informative consultation with the head of my brother's transplant team reassured me: diet, exercise, and level of activity can all remain the same after a recovery period. Although we have two kidneys, neither one operates at its full potential. If one kidney does shut down, the other is able to take over and function for both. By donating a kidney, I would not be giving up half of what I needed; my other kidney would compensate for the loss and begin to operate at full capacity.

At the end of the screening process, the transplant team determined that my youngest brother was the best donor, and he gave the gift of a kidney to our ailing brother.

■

Kidneys and the spiritual life. What do they have in common? Sometimes I look at my life in the same way I looked at my kidney. If I give away some of what I have, whether it be spiritually or emotionally, I fear that I will have that much less for myself. Does this sound familiar?

The reality is that we will never know how much we are truly capable of giving and the extent to which God has filled our lives until we give some away. Not until we meet the needs of another do we find out how much we have within us to give. The following meditation passage from the Gospel of Luke tells us that as we give, so shall we receive. If we are self-concerned and stingy in our giving, we will not receive much in return from the Lord. If we freely give to God and others, God will lavish his abundance upon us.

Some years ago I spent every Sunday night praying with individuals for healing and other spiritual needs. Almost invariably I would approach Sunday evening with some dread, fearing that I was committed to give more spiritual and emotional energy than I believed I possessed at the time. But by the end of the prayer session, even though I was tired, I found myself more spiritually and emotionally energized than I ever anticipated I could be. God moved *in* to fill my need as I moved *out* to meet others' needs.

We can be generous toward God and toward others because we know that God will be generous toward us. Let's not pass up opportunities to reach out to others and to give of ourselves. Let's not avoid a sacrifice of our time, energy, or attention because we fear that we will not have enough left over. God, who is generous and faithful in all things, will fill us to overflowing with a greater abundance than we could ever imagine. But God will not move *in* until we move *out*.

For Personal Reflection and Response
Do you try to protect yourself from others out of fear of not having enough for yourself? The next time you perform some act of service or kindness to another, reflect on your experience. Even though it may have been tiring, did you feel more depleted or did you experience renewed energy?

Scripture for Meditation

Give, and it will be given to you. A good measure, pressed down, shaken together and running over, will be poured into your lap; for the measure you give will be the measure you get back.

LUKE 6:38

14

From the Inside Out

Back on our farm in Michigan, we had a huge old apple tree just outside the kitchen window. The previous owners of the home boasted that this apple tree was the second-largest-diameter apple tree in the county. I believed it. The tree, three feet across, had been there for close to a hundred years and looked as if it would stand for another hundred. So I was rather surprised one morning, after a particularly strong storm, to see that a large section of the tree had blown down. As much as I hated to do it, I was forced to cut down the rest of it.

I wasn't looking forward to the task, because the girth of the tree made my eighteen-inch chain saw look inadequate. After a couple of minutes of cutting, I was surprised to find that the resistance on the saw had lessened considerably. Puzzled, I continued cutting. Eventually I got to a point where I was able to get a better look. By the time the tree was completely on the ground, it was clear that only about an inch and a half around the circumference of the tree was actually solid. The entire inside of the tree was hollow.

As I thought about that tree, I realized how

deceiving appearances can be. Externally that tree seemed to be a massive, strong tree— nothing wrong with it. One would never have guessed that the inside was empty.

■

Reflecting on that tree makes me think of what I call look-good Christianity. Look-good believers are those who do all of the right things so that they look like committed, sincere Christians. Internally, however, things are not as solid as the outside would suggest. The inside of look-good Christians is often just as hollow as the inside of that old apple tree. With the apple tree, the inside slowly died off either from disease or age.

With look-good Christians, it is not that things deteriorate with age, but rather that these people place such importance on the externals that they never take time to ensure that things internally are healthy and strong. Being humble, compassionate, learning how to not judge others—these are more important to true Christian growth and maturity than the obvious external practices in which a person may engage.

Unfortunately we like to measure things by what we can see and feel. This is what makes look-good Christianity so appealing to people. We can appear to be growing in the Christian life, because we are doing things that can be measured and quantified. Our human nature wants to be assured that we are loved by the Lord and growing closer to him. So the temptation is to grab onto those things that can be most readily measured—the externals. My old apple tree had stopped real growth many years ago, even though it still put out leaves in the summer and bore some small, misshapen apples. Look-good Christians can seem to be bearing fruit. But the growth is marginal because the inside is not solid.

Today let us reflect upon where we have placed our focus in regard to spiritual growth. Are we growing internally, or is our focus on the externals? Are we missing the real growth in humility, kindness, compassion, and patience? It's not too late to work on these. Let's not allow an unexpected spiritual wind to blow us down.

For Personal Reflection and Response

After prayerful consideration, choose a virtue in which you need to grow (for example, patience, joy, self-control). Find one or more resources to help you, such as a book, a confessor, a trusted friend, or a family member. Pray for the Holy Spirit to help you grow in this virtue.

Scripture for Meditation

The fruit of the Spirit is love, joy, peace, patience, kindness, generosity, faithfulness, gentleness and self-control.

GALATIANS 5:22-23

15

Keep Paddling!

We stood on the bank, watching the river rush by. It was an awesome sight. We had come to do white-water rafting. The frequent spring rains coupled with heavy winter snow had swollen the river to its highest point in years. The park rangers had just opened the river to limited rafting with qualified outfitters.

Ours was the last raft to go out that morning, and we watched each raft ahead of us rush into the current and move swiftly downstream. As we came around the first curve, we could see a stretch of white water ahead of us. It was an incredible sight: water standing straight, slanting back against the current, and crashing into unseen rocks.

Suddenly the raft ahead of us, which was carrying teenagers, flipped into the air, spilling them into the foaming water.

After navigating the white water ourselves, we drew up against the bank and pulled one of the students out of the water. There were some very tense moments until all of them were accounted for. There had been eight in the raft, and two were trapped in an air pocket underneath the overturned raft and went quite a ways downstream before the outfitters were able to get them. The young woman we rescued sat in the center of our raft for the rest of the trip, terrified and miserable.

When she was finally able to talk, the young woman told us that when they had hit the white water they had become frightened and stopped paddling. When they had stopped paddling, they had lost what control they had and met with disaster. They had violated one of the cardinal rules of rafting: keep paddling! Only if rafters continue to paddle and maintain some control over the raft are they able to navigate white water.

■

Spiritually, we all hit white water now and then. Life is in turmoil and seems out of our control. We may find ourselves undergoing strong temptation. Perhaps prayer seems dry and lacks meaning for us. God seems distant, and we don't feel connected with him. Maybe Scripture reading becomes tedious; we no longer receive insight and a sense of direction from the Word. Sometimes the people we had been counting on let us down. Maybe something goes wrong in a relationship, and it becomes a source of distress and consternation. We may become confused about our life's direction. We ask, "Does God even care what I'm doing or where I'm going?"

What do you do when you hit spiritual white water? The temptation is to become confused and stop paddling; we stop doing things we know are important. At times of greatest stress, when we need prayer, Scripture, meditation, and personal support the most, we often feel least like pursuing them. Although we can't avoid spiritual white water, chances are that if we stop "paddling" we will be in even worse shape. To completely stop praying or reading Scripture when we are in trouble is an open invitation to greater disaster. Circumstances can flip us over and we spend a long, miserable time trying to dry out afterward. No matter how great the temptation is to give up, at that point we have to keep paddling, keep pressing on. Even though God may seem very far away and unavailable to us, he still gives us the strength and courage to continue on our course.

On the river each raft has a leader who sits on the back of the raft and steers. He's the one who calls out directions to paddle forward, backward, right, left, and so on. The Holy Spirit sits in the raft of our life helping to steer it. He looks ahead for the rocks and the white water. He calls out directions to us to get us through safely. The devil is also present, yelling, "Stop paddling. It's not doing any good. Nothing will save you now. You're doomed. This white water is more than you can handle. It's too much for you."

The high school students on our rafting trip chose to listen to the person who was shouting out panicky orders instead of to the experienced outfitter. They paid the price. When we hit life's white-water problems, the voices of panic, both from outside and inside, will grow loud. Let's look our fears straight in the eye, take courage, and trust in the raft master who is guiding us down the river. When we hit white water, paddle.

For Personal Reflection and Response
Do you have favorite Scripture passages that you turn to in times of trouble? If not, a Bible concordance can help you compile a short list of psalms and other verses that you can pray during times of spiritual confusion, stress, or dryness. Here are some suggestions to get you started: Psalm 13; Psalm 121; Hebrews 12:1-12; Revelation 3:11-13.

Scripture for Meditation
Finally, be strong in the Lord and in the strength of his power.... For our struggle is not against enemies of blood and flesh, but against the rulers, against the authorities, against the cosmic powers of this present darkness, against the spiritual forces of evil in the heavenly places.

EPHESIANS 6:10, 12

16
Are You Prepared for Death?

One of the most formative experiences of my life took place during college. I had a part-time job driving an ambulance for a mortuary. My job required that I sleep in an upstairs apartment of the mortuary three or four nights a week and respond to requests for ambulance service during the night.

My first night on the job we were called to a gruesome automobile accident. A drunk driver ran a red light and hit the passenger side of another car carrying two high school students. The male driver was bruised but OK. His girl-friend was not. We placed her in the ambulance and started to the hospital with the young man riding in the back of the ambulance with me. Speeding across town with lights flashing and siren blaring seemed like an eternity. As I sat there, I saw the shock and fear in the eyes of the young man. Something inside of me did a major shift. I realized that life indeed was very short. Like all young people, I believed that death was a long way off. Of course I had read newspaper accounts of young people dying, but not until I was in that ambulance looking at a young woman who might not live more than a few moments did the reality of the fleeting nature of life hit home.

■

In 1986 our sixteen-year-old son drowned while he and I were fishing. It was a tragedy of immense proportions for our family. None of us has been the same since that accident.

Tim did not expect to die that day. In fact, he had every reason to be looking toward the future. It was his birthday. He was fishing, something he loved to do. The two of us were spending quality time as father and son. And yet God saw fit to call him home that day.

The one consolation we have from that tragedy is the knowledge that Tim was ready to meet the Lord. He loved God. He had a sincere personal relationship with Jesus. Although he wasn't planning to die, he was, nevertheless, ready.

We find it hard to understand why these kinds of things happen, and we are grieved that loved ones and friends are taken from us at such an early age. When we are young, we are filled with a certain sense of indestructibility. Tragedy, crippling illness, death, they all seem far away and part of another world. We think that now is not the time to worry about those things. "Hey, life is good. Let's not worry about tomorrow." But we should take notice when the young die. We ought not to go on with life as usual. We should be shaken to our very roots. This is a time to examine our own lives and ask if we are ready to die. It is foolish to take a cavalier attitude, believing that "this can't happen to me."

Are we ready to die? Most of us probably are not. If we did die today would we be ready to face God? How many of us are living life on the edge right now? How many of us take the approach "I'll sin now and repent later"? Such an approach presumes that we are in charge of the time of our deaths. Nothing could be further from the truth. We do not determine when we will die. Our time of death is in God's hands. What is in our hands is the condition we will be in when we die. Today we can start to reform those areas of life that are not under the lordship of Christ. To rationalize sin is to play Russian roulette with our eternal salvation. We should not trivialize those things that have eternal consequences. We can't avoid death, but we can be prepared for it.

For Personal Reflection and Response
Are you prepared for death? It may be helpful to make an inventory of your life and note which areas need reform. Perhaps a general confession is in order and a talk with a confessor about how to avoid serious sin.

Scripture for Meditation
Yet you do not even know what tomorrow will bring. What

is your life? For you are a mist that appears for a little while and then vanishes.

JAMES 4:14

17

God's Handprint

The best place to fish a stream is often the hardest to get to. This is the case with fishing for brook trout in northern Michigan. Some of the biggest brookies are found in brush-choked streams that can be reached only by a long, hard walk.

Once, while trying to get to one of these streams, I was forcing my way through a tangle in the woods. Suddenly, I heard a loud crash, a splash, and then silence. This was black bear country, and I suspected that I had spooked a bear not too far ahead of me. Arriving at the stream, I didn't see a bear, but when I looked down on the bank I noticed a large bear print slowly filling with water. I could no longer hear the bear or see him, but I knew from his print that he had indeed just passed this way. As I fished that day, I listened hard with both ears and kept one eye constantly on the bank.

■

In the incarnation of Jesus, we see God. We don't see his full glory, but we see human flesh and blood. The glory of Christ's deity is hidden in his humanity. Nevertheless, those who saw Jesus saw God. The activity of Jesus among us for thirty-odd years was God's indication of his complete and total presence to us.

Since Jesus' resurrection and ascension, the world no

longer sees Christ in the flesh. We cannot touch him or speak to him or hear him, but he is with us. Christ left us tangible signs of his presence. Just as the bear left his print, so Christ leaves his imprint to let us know that he is present with us. We can see his imprint most clearly in the sacraments and Scripture. We can also see the mark of Christ in the glorious colors of a beautiful sunrise or sunset. The way that nature goes through her changes of season—and the colors, sights, smells, and sounds that go with each season—are a sign of the presence and the goodness of the Lord. Good friends reveal his presence to us. The many blessings in our lives let us know that God is very near.

Often our temptation is to look for big, loud, splashing things to announce God's presence. Such things do happen to some of the saints: The curé of Ars was thrown around the room by the devil; Margaret Mary Alacoque had profound visions of Christ; Teresa of Avila levitated; others heard audible voices or received visions of heaven or hell; still others performed astounding healings and miracles. We believe that those types of manifestations are the surest signs of God's love for us, so we look and hope for audible voices, goose bumps, or a sense of mystery to assure us that God is indeed with us.

Sometimes these things happen, but most often they don't. God's ordinary way of being with us and speaking to us is through the daily happenings in our lives: a quiet half hour of Scripture reading or a brief stop at a church; a pleasant conversation with a good friend; a walk in the park with the sun shining and a gentle breeze blowing. An afternoon or evening of serious study in the library can be an experience of the presence of God.

Sometimes unpleasant experiences are also signs of God's presence, such as a gentle rebuke or correction from a friend or confessor. Dealing with a difficult interpersonal situation can force us to look at the person in a new light, and we can see Christ there.

Let's explore the ways God has already revealed himself to us. A grateful, thankful spirit opens us to receive even more awareness of God's presence.

For Personal Reflection and Response

Which ordinary activities, places, or experiences have drawn you close to God? Have you ever thanked him for those experiences?

Try to spend some time this week engaged in a place where or in activity in which or you experience the presence of God. Remember to thank him for this sign of his love for you.

Scripture for Meditation

Long ago God spoke to our ancestors in many and various ways by the prophets, but in these last days he has spoken to us by his Son, whom he appointed heir of all things, through whom he also created the world. He is the reflection of God's glory and the exact imprint of God's very being, and he sustains all things by his powerful word.

HEBREWS 1:1-3

18

But I Don't Deserve It

One day while I was in seventh grade, my friend and I were outside the school building in late afternoon after the other students had gone home. A soda truck pulled up, and the driver began loading cases of soda onto a dolly to take into the school cafeteria to replenish the coolers. As he headed for the school door, he looked at the two of us staring wide-eyed at all the cases of soda and said, "If you guys will keep an eye on this truck for me, I will give each of you a free soda when I am finished here." This was too good to be true. All we had to do was stand there, watch the truck, and get a free soda.

I had been taught that a person was supposed to work for things, so I found it hard to believe that something really good could happen to someone who hadn't earned it. As the trucker unloaded his last cases and took them into the school, I felt uncomfortable about just waiting for the soda he promised us. I moved over to the side of the school building, where I was half out of sight. When the trucker came back, my friend was right there with his hand out, eager and fully expectant that the truck driver was going to make good on his promise. The truck driver looked around and said, "Where's your friend? Doesn't he want one?" Feeling very shy, I came out from behind the building, and we both got a free bottle of soda.

At first glance it may seem both strange and humorous that a seventh grader would be shy about receiving a gift of soda from someone. But something inside of me instinctively rebelled against the notion that I had any *right* to this free bottle of soda, because I had done nothing to *earn* it. It never occurred to me that the truck driver simply enjoyed giving it as a free gift. (Nor did I think that I might have been serving some useful purpose as a watchman.)

God has given us incomprehensibly valuable gifts: Christ's resurrection is the promise of our own; as a down payment on that promise, the Lord gives us another gift, that of the Holy Spirit. There is nothing we could ever do to earn or deserve these gifts. But some of us have trouble freely receiving them. We may accept these gifts intellectually, but emotionally we still believe that we need to do something to deserve them.

God's love, which causes him to lavish such gifts upon us, so transcends us that no amount of good actions, pious thoughts, or holy words can ever merit what he gives us. When we recognize and accept our unworthiness before God, we can then bask in the vastness of God's love and gifts. Only as we accept our own position are we able to finally, fully, and freely accept what God wants lovingly to give us. This experience of God's love has been the motivating factor for the heroic lives of the saints over the centuries. Men and women who understood and accepted the incredible love God had for them found that they could not help but return that love in obedience and service for the rest of their lives.

God's love is a transforming love. It sweeps away the old and makes possible all kinds of *new*. God's love is a purifying love that burns out our self-centeredness and makes it possible for us to love other people. God's love is an embracing love. It enables us to reach beyond ourselves and touch others no matter how different they may be from us. We can reach out to those whom we would not ordinarily be attracted to, those who believe, think, act, and dress differently than we do. God's love is a freeing love. It enables us to move beyond the boundaries of self, to be channels of God's mercy to others. We are able to put ourselves in others' shoes and see life through their eyes. We are able to shake free from the chains of self that bind us to our own little worldview and to see things from God's perspective. God's love is a forgiving love that enables us to treat all people with the same level of respect, mercy, and forgiveness that we have experienced from God.

Take this opportunity to reflect upon and appropriate the vastness of God's freely given love. Let's not hide behind walls of timidity or false humility. Get out there next to the soda truck and hold out your hand.

For Personal Reflection and Response

Think about gifts you have given to people you love. Did you ask yourself whether the person deserved it before you gave the gift?

Prayerfully confront your own feelings of unworthiness that keep you from receiving God's love. Release each feeling into God's hands. You may wish to recite the following Scripture verse from Romans as you do so.

Scripture for Meditation

He who did not withhold his own Son, but gave him up for all of us, will he not with him also give us everything else?

ROMANS 8:32

19

Paid in Full

"Fifty cents!?" The New York cabbie looked at me with a mixture of incredulity and disgust. "Fifty cents!? Where are you from anyway, boy?"

"M-M-Michigan," I stammered.

"What's the matter? Don't they tip in Michigan?" roared the cabbie. My first encounter with a New York cab driver was becoming an emotional experience for both of us.

I was twenty-two years old, had been in a taxicab one other time in my life, and had no idea how tipping worked. The total amount of the cab fare was between ten and twelve dollars. I opened my wallet and found the exact amount of money for the fare without having to break a larger bill, and I had two quarters at hand for the tip. As I gave him my fifty-cent tip, I told him in a suave and sophisticated manner, "Here, this is for you."

The explosive reaction of the driver drew the attention of the hotel doorman, the porter, and other people who stopped to watch the scene unfold. Embarrassed and uncomfortable, I grabbed my wallet again, looked inside, and saw only twenty-dollar bills. I ran into the hotel, got change for a twenty, and blindly thrust a wad of bills into the cabbie's hand. He got away with most of the twenty dollars. He was still telling me what he thought of me as he pulled away from the curb. My new bride, my "helpmate," who was from the New York area, was no help at all. She thought the whole thing was hilarious.

■

We often find ourselves in situations or circumstances where our usual way of doing things is insufficient for the new surroundings. Trying to deal with the world, the flesh, and the devil out of our own resources is similar to what I experienced with the New York cab driver: totally inadequate. The world, the flesh, and the devil make big demands on us. They seem to yell and scream with great intensity, trying to force us to deal with them on their terms. But when we do, we are out of our league. What we need is a totally new way of understanding our situation. This comes from the death and resurrection of Christ.

Because of Jesus' death and resurrection, we are new people, and the world, the flesh, and the devil no longer have a claim on us. Don't be deceived by the uproar they create. In Christ, the full fare was paid, a huge tip was given, and there is no longer anything that can be demanded of us. Our struggle has become easier because of Christ's death. It is not completely over, but it has become easier. As we understand the reality of the resurrection in our lives and allow that reality to penetrate more of our thinking and our actions, we will find that we have a new ability to deal with things that we previously found difficult to handle.

In the Book of Revelation Jesus says, "See, I am making all things new" (21:5). We will not see the full completion of this until the second coming of Christ, but even now everything is different, everything has a new meaning because of the resurrection of Jesus.

New situations call for new responses. New York City cab drivers call for a different response than Muskegon, Michigan, cab drivers. We have a new life because of Christ. We live now in the Holy Spirit. The fare has been fully paid.

For Personal Reflection and Response

What sin or habit are you trying to overcome? Are you using your own willpower to deal with it? Is it working? Meditating on the power and love of Christ as expressed in his resurrection can enable you to see the problem in a new light of faith and hope.

The following prayer can help you keep your eyes fixed on the source of your strength:

Lord, by your cross and resurrection you have set me free. I believe your power is at work in my life. Give me the faith, courage, and strength to overcome this problem.

Scripture for Meditation

If the Spirit of him who raised Jesus from the dead dwells in you, he who raised Christ from the dead will

give life to your mortal bodies also through his Spirit
that dwells in you.

ROMANS 8:11

20

We Have to Stand Up

I was mostly underwater, gripping the towrope
for dear life. My knees were pushed back to my
ears and the water coming from between the
skis was hitting me in the face. This was not the
dazzling display of waterskiing I had anticipated. Eventually my arms got tired, and I let go
of the towrope. The boat circled around and
came up next to me. My friends, between guf-
faws, told me that when the towrope started to
pull me, I was supposed to work with the pull
and stand up on the skis. We tried it again. This
time as I felt the resistance against the skis, I
stood up on the skis, weight toward my heels. Lo
and behold, I was waterskiing. It wasn't pretty,
but I was waterskiing.

Based on my casual observations of other
people waterskiing and the little instruction that
I received before I tried it, I assumed that the
boat did the work and all I had to do was hang
onto the towrope. To a large extent, that was
true. The boat did have the power, the towrope
enabled it to pull me, and the skis were designed
to glide over the top of the water. The boat, rope,
and skis were all doing their part, but I needed
to do my part for skiing to happen. When the
boat pulled, I needed to stand up on the skis.

Once I did that, all the elements were working together. I took off across the lake.

■

We know that we need to rely on the power of the Holy Spirit to live the Christian life. We cannot do it on our own. Confident of this, some of us make the mistake of assuming that the power of the Holy Spirit will do it all. Just as I had to stand up so my skis would function in harmony with the power of the boat, so too in the Christian life, we need to "stand up" and work in harmony with the Holy Spirit.

The Spirit has the power to deliver us from sinful habits and inclinations. But he will never be able to deliver us from pornography, for example, if we continue to view pornography. He cannot deliver us from drunkenness if we continue to drink alcohol. If we want God's power to help us overcome a problem with lying, we have to start using our mouth to tell the truth. For students, praying harder, saying rosaries or novenas, or engaging in other laudable spiritual activities is no substitute for study to achieve academic success. The Holy Spirit can't help with our studies if we don't seriously study.

We have to do our part to accept and actuate the power of God. When Jesus healed the blind man, as recounted in chapter nine of the Gospel of John, he spit on the ground, made mud, and rubbed it in the man's eyes. Then he told him to go and wash his face in the pool of Siloam. The man went to the pool, washed, and was able to see. If he had not gone to the pool and washed his face, would he have been healed? Probably not. His eyes would have been covered with mud made from Jesus' spit, but he would not have received his sight. He needed to do his part—act on his faith.

Whatever our need, we must work in tandem with God to deal with it. Not everything works out as we wish. It's a mystery why we overcome some difficulties and not others. Regardless of the outcome, it is clear that if we do not stand up on those skis and cooperate with the power of God, we will not overcome anything.

For Personal Reflection and Response

Think of one sinful habit or inclination you would like to overcome. What specific action can you take that will indicate that you are working in tandem with God's power to overcome this problem?

Scripture for Meditation

Jesus...said to me, "Go to Siloam and wash." Then I went and washed and received my sight.

JOHN 9:11

21

Heel!

I stood in front of the dog kennel, training collar in one hand, training leash in the other, watching the two dogs. One was crouched, incontinent, in the corner of the kennel. The other was eagerly jumping against the gate, waiting to be let out. I was training my two young dogs to obey basic commands. These dogs were about as different from one another as night and day. Digger, a golden retriever, was the runt of his litter. He was nervous, high-strung and very sensitive. Dusty, a female, tan Labrador retriever was muscular, aggressive, playful, and eager for any type of challenge.

I was training the dogs to heel. This is a position the dog takes just outside of and slightly behind the trainer's left leg. This allows the dog to pay maximum attention to what the trainer is doing. If I stop, the dog can stop; if I turn right, the dog turns right; if I turn left, so does the dog. The goal of this position is to establish an intimate communication relationship between the trainer and the animal.

Being a novice dog trainer, I started out with great confidence and enthusiasm but soon found myself in a quandary. The things that worked for the headstrong, impulsive, free-ranging Dusty, did not work for the shy, timid Digger.

Dusty needed a firm hand. She seemed to enjoy knowing there was strength and purpose in what I was doing with her. I needed to use a loud voice to bring her back and to help her understand my other commands. And little by little she was responding to this form of training.

Digger, on the other hand, became frightened if I spoke in a loud voice. He quivered, nearly immobilized, when he hit the end of the leash and felt the collar pinch. His personality couldn't handle it. Our training sessions were no longer fun for Digger.

As I stood outside the kennel that morning and watched Digger shiver in the corner, I realized I would need to take an entirely different approach with him. I took a gentler hand and spoke in a soothing voice: Digger responded better and quicker than he had previously. Both dogs were finally trained. Both turned out to be excellent in their own ways, but I needed to use two different methods.

■

As I trained these dogs, I learned something about the spiritual life. I was struck by the parallel between a dog's learning to heel with a trainer and our learning to "heel" with the Lord. Jesus wants us to have a loving and trusting relationship with him. You could say that we should be walking in relationship to the Lord the same way that a trained dog walks in relationship to its trainer, just a half step behind and right up close. That way, we can see when he stops, when he turns right, when he turns left, or when he goes faster. We will have our eyes on him, paying attention to what he does.

Heeling does not come naturally to dogs or humans. We have the same tendency as my young dogs, to run whichever way we want, get into mischief, and come back to the kennel when we want. The Lord is an expert trainer. He knows how to train each of us. He knows our particular personality and background. He knows what is in our heart because he made each of us.

Sometimes his training may not make sense to us. We may not understand why he seems to treat us differently from someone else. But his goal for each of us is the same: loving union with him. To be brought into this relationship, some of us need a firm hand, others a gentler one. Our job is to respond as Digger and Dusty did by paying attention to the trainer and knowing that it is for our own good. Eventually we will be in the position he wants: at his side, slightly behind, keeping our eyes on him. Tugging at the collar, biting at the leash, running to the end of the line every time we get a chance, sitting down, digging in our heels, trying to go our own way will simply prolong our training period and make it more painful and frustrating.

As trained dogs come to know, the most comfortable, reassuring, safe, and pleasant place is at the heel position.

After all, the dog just wants to be near his master, and the heel position is as near as he can get. Let's not fight the Lord's training. The heel position is the happiest place for us.

For Personal Reflection and Response
If you can find a book or, better yet, a video on basic dog training, you might find it both entertaining and instructive. As you study the relationship between the trainer and the dog, notice any lessons that can be applied to your relationship with Christ, especially how the dog learns to trust the trainer completely.

Scripture for Meditation
[God] disciplines us for our good, in order that we may share in his holiness. Now, discipline always seems painful rather than pleasant at the time, but later it yields the peaceful fruit of righteousness to those who have been trained by it.

HEBREWS 12:10-11

22
He Didn't Look "Right"

I couldn't believe it. There stood Leonard wearing patched, old waders, a crumpled railroad cap on his head, an ancient spinning rod in his hand, and a bait box full of worms over his shoulder.

Our family was camping in the Upper Peninsula of Michigan. One reason we chose this campsite was that I wanted to go fly-fishing on a famous stretch of the Two-Hearted River. One evening as Therese and I sat around our fire, our kids finally asleep in the tent,

Leonard and Lottie (the only other people in the campground) came over to chat. The talk turned to fishing; they were both avid trout fishermen. Leonard and I decided to go fishing the next day.

The next morning I showed up, looking like an ad for some upscale fly-fishing magazine, only to come face to face with Leonard, who looked anything but upscale. A great deal of skepticism arose in my mind as to whether Leonard really knew what he was doing. After some discussion, Leonard convinced me that my fly rod would be useless on this brush-choked stream. So I traded in my fancy equipment for a spinning rod and a box of worms.

I became even more skeptical as I watched Leonard's fishing technique. He was doing everything wrong. He waded downstream instead of upstream. He walked right up to where fish would be feeding and dropped the worm on top of them. All my fishing experience led me to believe that this technique would result in failure.

We parted to fish. Leonard went the wrong way (downstream), and I walked the right way (upstream). Carefully approaching each likely looking spot, I cast my worm in from a distance, letting it bounce down with the natural flow of the stream—doing everything by the book. When we met up again a few hours later, Leonard had a creel full of brook trout. I had nothing.

In fact, in all the years we fished together, Leonard always caught more fish than I. He was a happier fisherman, too, and quite content with his own method of fishing. In the end, I learned a lot from Leonard, a guy who did everything "wrong."

■

Judging people by appearances is an occupational hazard for us human beings. We tend to get caught up in the externals and lose sight of the more important matters of the heart. Judging others is an insidious sin with disastrous consequences both for us and for those we judge. It is insidious because we climb onto God's judgment seat and set a new standard for people—usually an external one that has little to do with the underlying realities of another person's life.

It has disastrous consequences, because when we put ourselves in God's place we have the mistaken notion that we see things the way God does. A judgmental attitude has further disastrous consequences, because we don't give ourselves a chance to appreciate what is good and valuable in another person.

Do we find ourselves judging others because of the clothes they wear or don't wear? Do we judge others because they don't share our view of what is proper music or our understanding of how to walk, talk, eat, or pray? What about those who do not engage in the same kind of devotions as we do or those who genuflect or don't genuflect, bow or don't bow before receiving Communion?

There is a difference between judgment and a judgmental spirit. Judgment is a gift of the Holy Spirit that enables *us* to discern what is the good *we* ought to do in each situation. A judgmental spirit is a work of the flesh that presumes to assess the motives or the purity of heart of *another*. The judgmental person decides who is righteous and who is not. Let's not judge others by external appearances but see people with the heart of Christ. Let's keep our eyes focused on our own sins and our own faults.

Leonard, who wore ratty old waders and used second-hand equipment, was a much better fisherman than I.

Remember him the next time you are tempted to judge someone by appearances. That person may very well be a much better follower of Christ than you.

For Personal Reflection and Response
Is a judgmental spirit at work in your life? Is there someone toward whom you are particularly judgmental? Try praying for that person each day, not that he or she will change what you don't like but rather that God will greatly bless him or her. As you pray, ask God to open your eyes to see the good qualities in that person.

Scripture for Meditation
Do not judge by appearances, but judge with right judgment.

JOHN 7:24

Do not judge, and you will not be judged; do not condemn, and you will not be condemned. Forgive, and you will be forgiven.

LUKE 6:37-38

23

The Grass Isn't Greener

The goat wouldn't stop bleating. I knew what the problem was, and I knew what I had to do. I was just reluctant to get out of bed and go outdoors in the middle of the night. I didn't have much choice. I couldn't get back to sleep; the goat was practically outside our bedroom window, its head caught in the fence.

We were caring for a small herd of goats. They

frequently decided that the grass in our neighbor's pasture looked much better than whatever they were eating in ours. The fence between the pastures was designed for cows and horses, not for goats. The openings between the strands of wire were just large enough for the goats to slip their heads through. But then they had a problem. Sticking out from the top of their heads and angling back were two small, six-inch horns. When a goat slid its head through the fence, the horns helped push aside the wire strands. But when the goat tried to pull its head back out, the horns caught in the fence. Consequently the goat would bleat and struggle until someone freed it. This was not an easy task, because the goat had no idea why it was caught in the fence and could not understand that it needed to hold still until the wire strands could be pulled apart.

None of us liked the job of freeing the goats from the fence. Pinched fingers, bruised arms, and sore toes were the usual reward. Freeing a goat one day, I said, "You stupid goat. Every time you stick your head through the fence, you get caught. Look at all the nice pasture on this side of the fence. Eat this, and you'll be happy."

When the owner made other arrangements and finally moved the goats to a different farm, you had better believe that our entire family rejoiced.

■

We are a lot like that goat. God has placed us in an excellent pasture, but we keep looking through the fence at the pasture of the world. The grass in the world's pasture can look very tasty. So we stick our heads through the fence to eat "just a little bit" of the world's grass, and then we want to get back to God's pasture. But lo and behold, the devil's fence is just big enough to get through and not quite big enough to get back out. The horns of our flesh get us into the world but then hinder us when we try to retreat.

The combination of the world, the flesh, and the devil entice us to stick our heads into places we shouldn't be, and we get caught. Then we begin to bleat and carry on, asking God to get us out of the predicament. Fortunately, the Lord is a much more patient and considerate herdsman than I was. He hears our moaning and our bleating, pulls apart the devil's fence, and puts us back into good pasture. Then he looks at us and says, "Silly goat, this is the best pasture for you. Stay here."

We are content for a while. We promise ourselves that we won't make the mistakes again. But then we seem to forget our past experiences. We feed closer and closer to the fence. The next thing we know, our heads are through and we are caught again.

The world's pasture is very enticing. Certain people, opportunities, situations, and places appear to be lots of fun and very freeing. They appeal to us. We find ourselves being drawn to things we know, ultimately, are not going to be good for us.

When we do get caught, yes, let's cry out to the Lord and ask for his help and expect him to help us. But keep in mind that God is not at our beck and call. He is not in the business of protecting us from all the consequences of our choices and actions. We may experience pain and difficulties that are meant to teach us the lesson of not sticking our heads through the fence again. God has given us plenty of good pasture. Let's stay on his side of the fence and feast on the good things he has provided for us.

For Personal Reflection and Response
What attractions of the world draw you away from God—
music, friends, activities?

How can you prevent being caught by them? Perhaps
the best way is to avoid them. How can you do this?

Scripture for Meditation
The iniquities of the wicked ensnare them,
    and they are caught in the toils of their sin.

PROVERBS 5:22

24

He Gives Sight to the Blind

It had been a long, hard morning of deer hunting.
The day was cold. The sky was gray and over-
cast, and only a dim light filtered through the
woods. I had neither heard nor seen a deer the
entire morning. I approached a small hollow
where I hoped to find some and very carefully
examined the entire area. After a few moments I
thought I saw some small movement. Staring
hard at the spot, I thought it was a log on the
ground with branches sticking up. I continued to
stare and decided it was a deer with a nice rack of
antlers. I reconsidered. No, it was just a log with
branches sticking up. I had been hunting fruit-
lessly all morning, and I really wanted this to be
a deer. The longer I stared at it, the more convinced I became that it was. Because there was no
way I could get to a place for a decent shot without spooking the deer and losing him completely,
I could only wait until the deer decided to move.

The afternoon wore on, and the deer didn't

move. Every time I was tempted to believe that this was just a log, I thought my eyes detected some slight movement that made it a deer. I became very cold, cramped, and hungry.

Toward late afternoon, my hunting partner walked up behind me. When I told him about the deer in the hollow, he pulled out his binoculars, took a look, and handed them to me. With the binoculars I was able to see clearly. I had been waiting all afternoon for a log to move.

■

I had deceived myself into seeing a deer that wasn't there. That's the trouble with wanting something to be the way *we* want it to be. We allow ourselves to believe something that isn't true.

This "seeing" problem is not limited to our physical eyes. We can have this same problem with our spiritual eyes. We know that certain activities are objectively wrong, such as sex between people who are not married to each other. But if we look at the issue long enough, believing that perhaps in this case or with this person it really isn't all that wrong, we convince ourselves that it's OK because we now "see" it differently. We know that drunkenness is wrong. But because we had a long, hard week or something bad has happened to us, and we feel a little sorry for ourselves, we see getting drunk in a different light.

The Lord has provided the sacrament of reconciliation for us so that we can receive forgiveness as well as grace and strength to overcome temptation in the future. The sacrament helps us to see our sin and weakness in true light; it sharpens the eyes of our spirits so that we don't deceive ourselves about what is really sin.

Let the Lord touch your spiritual eyes so that you

can see clearly. What things are you "seeing" that need to be viewed through the clear lens of the Lord's perspective? We need the Lord's help to avoid self-deception, so we can live the full life in the Spirit that Christ offers to us. Let's not walk in the gray light of self-deception, but rather in the clear light of the Spirit of Christ.

For Personal Reflection and Response
What sins or bad habits have you managed to "see" as not all that wrong? After some reflection, you may feel the need to go to confession. You can also ask the Holy Spirit to help keep your spiritual eyesight sharp.

Scripture for Meditation
Once more Jesus put his hands on the man's eyes. Then his eyes were opened, sight was restored, and he saw everything clearly.

MARK 8:25

There is a way that seems right to a person,
     but its end is the way to death.

PROVERBS 14:12

———

25

What Would Your Mother Say?

It must have been a slow summer. First, we did something stupid: we decided to have a BB-gun war. We sat around for a couple of hours, choosing comrades and enemies and setting up the rules (no shooting at the head, only at protected areas of the body; you have to admit that you have been hit—an unenforceable rule for ten-year-olds). Then we did something really stupid. We had the war. All of us swore to secrecy (this was not the sort of thing you told your mother) and headed for the woods.

So there I was hiding behind a tree. I saw someone run between trees and started to take aim when suddenly I felt a sting in my upper shoulder right where the stock of the gun was nestled. One of the guys yelled, "Got you, Cirner!"

Yes, he had hit me and on a protected part of my body. The problem was that he had missed my eye by two inches. I had been so completely hidden by the tree that the only thing he could see was my arm and a little piece of my face. He had aimed at the only protected part he could find. If he had been poor marksman, or less lucky, I would have lost an eye. As I realized what I had just dodged, I knew that this playful little war had not been such a good idea after all. Our collective ten-year-old "wisdom" was, in fact, folly. The near miss sobered all of us, and we called a halt to the war. We often reminisced about the great BB-gun war, but nobody ever suggested that we do it again.

◼

How many times have we thought about taking stupid risks in our lives? What about using drugs or sexual experimentation outside of marriage? What about telling lies to avoid getting into trouble or gossiping about other people or trying to hide things for which we should take responsibility? Such thinking is pretty stupid in and of itself. But then we rationalize how we can actually do what we want: "I'll drink only two beers. I'll take only a couple of hits on this joint. I'll just tell this one lie, but I'll never do it again." We think we have ourselves covered by the "rules" we have set up. Then we do the really stupid thing. We engage in the behavior.

We really don't have control over what is going to happen once we set certain forces in motion. Even though our BB-gun war was carefully circumscribed with rules about where to aim, I had absolutely no control over where a BB would actually go. Nor could I control what other people would do. I put myself in the hands of kids who had demonstrated as much wisdom as I by agreeing to this fight in the first place.

We put ourselves at great risk when we entrust ourselves into the hands of others with behavior that jeopardizes our spiritual walk with the Lord. How do we know that the people we are with will support drinking only two beers? How do we know that this person will respect the sexual limits we have set? Can we control another's raging hormones? Once we are high, how will we control how many hits we will take?

As ten-year-olds planning a BB-gun war, we were not smart enough to know that we couldn't trust one another. But we did know that what we were doing was not right. That is why we didn't tell our mothers. Similarly, we know that engaging in risky or sinful behavior is not the right thing to do. But we seldom discuss our plans with anybody who has the wisdom and understanding to fully comprehend the situation because we know they would try to talk us out of it. So we talk only to other people who are just as stupid ourselves and our "collective wisdom" enables us to do what we want.

Losing an eye for the sake of a two-hour BB-gun war is hardly worth it. Losing one's virginity before marriage for the sake of temporary passion is pointless. Getting addicted to drugs for some fleeting good feelings or being known as untrustworthy because we lie is hardly worth the momentary pleasure or sense of safety that we get in engaging in the behavior. Ultimately it is harmful and destructive.

We can talk ourselves into doing just about anything. The next time you want to talk yourself into something sinful or irresponsible, ask yourself: What would Jesus say? What would a spiritual advisor say? Don't wait to learn the hard way. Sometimes we are warned by a near miss, but other times we are not afforded that luxury. We take a direct hit and the lives of many people get ruined in the process. It isn't worth it.

For Personal Reflection and Response

Relationships based on trust are important. Identify a person you know whom you trust to encourage you to do what is right. Consider speaking to that person about areas of your life that seem confusing. Ask for advice. Perhaps the two of you can agree to be of support to each other.

Scripture for Meditation

Listen to advice and accept instruction,
   that you may gain wisdom for the future.

PROVERBS 19:20

26

Think Like Your Quarry

"Ya gotta think like your quarry." I no longer remember which of the old-timers with whom I used to hunt and fish first told me this, but it is the best piece of advice a novice can get. However, it is easier said than done, and a misunderstanding of this little phrase has led to many humorous and embarrassing outdoor moments for me. For example, one opening day of deer season, I spent hours sitting in a little hollow with absolutely no cover, because I thought if I were a deer this would be a really comfortable place to bed down. Good idea, wrong animal. I was thinking what I would do if I were a deer rather than understanding what a deer would do in this situation.

Some years later on another opening day, my accumulated knowledge and experience of deer habits led to a different ending. After a fruitless morning I sat down and took stock. Remembering the physical layout of the area, I believed that a deer might be attracted to a particular stand of cedars with lots of cover. I cautiously moved toward the cedars. About thirty yards from the cedar stand, I saw a large buck coming off the ridge heading right to the cedars. I saw him a split second before he saw me, and that is why he is now mounted and hanging in my office.

■

Just as successful hunters need to think like and understand their quarry, so too success in our relationships as Christians often requires our being able to get into the mind of the other person.

Have you ever been unable to resolve a conflict with someone else? It may seem as if you are simply talking at each other, reiterating your own point of view. Or have you intended to help or serve someone, only to find that the person did not experience what you did as helpful? Perhaps you took it upon yourself to give someone advice only to find that your wonderful pearl of wisdom was not only unappreciated but summarily dismissed.

Good relationships among Christians are based on

more than knowledge of the truth, good theology, and a common understanding of Scripture. Good relationships flow from what we know of the other person and from our understanding of what that person needs at the moment.

Jesus came to us in human form, as a man, to relate to us in a way that we could understand. His human presence said to us, "I understand you and I know what you are going through because I am experiencing the same things." His word, although eternally true no matter how he chose to reveal it, was more powerful and effective because of the personal way Jesus brought it to us.

Our lives, our messages, our service, our love and affection for others ought to be presented in the same fashion as Jesus'. To do so, we must put ourselves in the other person's place and, before we act, see life as much as possible through that person's eyes.

For Personal Reflection and Response
Identify someone you would like to know better. Try to recognize what the person experiences as love and service and meet that person in his or her frame of reference this week through some service or act of kindness.

Scripture for Meditation
An intelligent mind acquires knowledge,
   and the ear of the wise seeks knowledge.

PROVERBS 18:15

27
Blowing in the Wind

Hour by hour, day by day the warbler's nest came together. As I watched from the kitchen window, I doubted at times that the nest would survive the strong winds, pounding rain, wet snow, and feathered thieves that challenged the process. One particularly windy day just about every piece of material the warblers collected was blown away, prompting them to scurry after it. The birds were pretty creative in finding building materials: dead grass and weeds, small twigs, string, even some tinsel caught in the weeds after Christmas.

Over the years I had collected enough old birds' nests for my kids to fill a small room, but I had never seen the building process up close. Somewhere in the back of my mind I imagined that when birds decided to move into a neighborhood they contracted with a local bird nest construction company. These little warblers unhinged that fantasy. Through patient perseverance, using one bit of material at a time, they completed the nest in about a week. Shortly after, three eggs appeared in it.

■

Growing in the spiritual life is a lot like building a bird's nest. Just as warblers don't buy a completed nest from Bird Nest Construction Co., neither can we buy a spiritual life that is complete and ready for us to move into. Our spiritual life is a relationship with Christ. It comes together bit by bit, piece by piece, hour by hour, day by day. It goes through all kinds of trials, tribulations, good times, bad times. My little warbler friends often had to work in extreme weather conditions, which helped guarantee that the nest would survive through upcoming bad weather.

Sometimes fierce spiritual winds and particularly difficult trials and tragedies batter our hard work. This is not the end of our growth. We pick up the pieces, work with them, and reassemble our relationship with Jesus. A spiritual life that is built only in and on good times is not going to be very strong. We want a spiritual life that will withstand the trials of time, the ups and downs of life.

The warblers did not build a nest by winding a long single strand of grass or string in a bowl-shaped configuration. Through careful manipulation and some bird spit, the warblers took bits and pieces of various materials and integrated them into an interdependent whole. Similarly our spiritual life is not supposed to comprise a long single strand of material. People who attempt a one-dimensional spiritual life soon find it inadequate. A better method involves patiently and persistently bringing together prayer, Scripture reading, meditation, the sacraments, loving relationships with other people, mercy works, and so on.

When the warblers' nest was finished, they moved in and raised nestlings. Our spiritual growth can progress to a point where we can "move in" and raise spiritual youngsters. That's not to say that our spiritual growth is ever finished; because God is infinite, we will never be finished developing a relationship with him. Our life on earth is just a start toward something that will continue forever.

Some birds need big nests; some birds need small nests. We shouldn't compare our own spiritual growth and development with that of anyone else. God calls each of us into profound relationship with him. We are patiently and persistently to bring together the bits and pieces that God gives us and put them together, in the power of the Holy Spirit, into a spiritual life that will carry us through good times as well as bad.

For Personal Reflection and Response
How would you characterize your spiritual life? Built by someone else and you are trying to live in it?

One-dimensional? Scattered? Coming together through hard work? Nonexistent?

If you would like to see some change, prioritize a short list of things you think you can do—or materials you can use—to strengthen your spiritual life. Start with your top item and slowly add the elements. After a while, your spiritual life will be much stronger and more integrated.

Scripture for Meditation

For this very reason, you must make every effort to support your faith with goodness, and goodness with knowledge, and knowledge with self-control and self-control with endurance, and endurance with godliness, and godliness with mutual affection, and mutual affection with love. For if these things are yours and are increasing among you, they keep you from being ineffective and unfruitful in the knowledge of our Lord Jesus Christ.

2 PETER 1:5-8

28

The Quick Path

I ached all over. I was bruised and bloody, lying on the ground at the foot of a "mountain," a case of crash and burn. "Are you OK?" an adult asked. As my brain cleared, I felt the first pangs of embarrassment and humiliation. Things had started out well, but I just didn't realize how steep the incline really was.

My family was visiting a well-known tourist attraction in Michigan, the Sleeping Bear Dunes. Using the stairway we climbed to the top, where we explored the sand dunes and enjoyed the beauty of Lake Michigan. When we kids grew restless, we all started the trek back down the steps. But, increasingly irritated at our slow pace, I looked for a way to speed up things. Alongside the steps I saw a narrow aisle that went right to the parking lot. So I took to the aisle and walked faster. After a couple of minutes I decided to ratchet this up another notch, faster. Before long I broke into a little trot. My trot turned into a lope, and before I realized it I was running wildly out of control down the mountain. I couldn't stop myself. My legs kept churning faster and faster as the force of gravity drew me down the dune. I hit the bottom and crashed into a heap in the dirt and gravel.

By the time the rest of my family arrived at the bottom, I knew I had nothing to say. I had done a stupid and dangerous thing. I acted before I realized the risks involved and the accident that was waiting to happen happened. Another painful lesson in my life.

It is tempting to wonder if we couldn't be having a better, more exciting life. The present path may seem dull, slow, and monotonous, while just off the path we see opportunity—freedom and possibility. Many of our sinful patterns or bad habits begin because we think we see a quick or more exciting route or a shortcut to some goal. We may think that taking drugs is a quick way to relax and have a good time. We may believe that lying is OK if it helps us advance in our career.

We may give sin or bad habits a try and find them exciting. When we don't get struck by lightning, when nothing terrible happens, we try a little bit more. We are gradually drawn more and more into such activity, until we suddenly find ourselves out of control. Just as gravity drew me faster and faster down the sand dune, so sin draws us faster and faster down its own path. Continuing to let sin have its way can ultimately have only one result: We crash and burn. Bruised and wounded, we wind up in a sorry heap.

In the act of contrition, we promise not only to avoid sin, but also to avoid the near occasions of sin. The near occasions of sin are those first steps we take off the path of righteousness and virtue. The near occasions draw us into patterns and habits that we find increasingly more difficult to break.

Unlike my little jaunt down Sleeping Bear Dunes, there is a way to stop our advance down the path of bad habits and sin. Every day, every moment, we have the opportunity to call upon Christ to help us. Without Christ's help, we are no match for sin. We have the sacraments, especially reconciliation and the Eucharist. We have the advice and counsel of others who can help us get off the slippery path and return to the solid way. Every day is a new beginning with the Lord and offers the possibility for walking the sure path that Christ walked before us—the path of holiness, peace, and contentment. Are we walking Christ's path, or are we running down the slope of sin?

For Personal Reflection and Response

Do you feel out of control in some part of your life? Does your life seem to be rushing forward on its own? A talk with a confessor or trusted friend may be just the thing you need to regain control. Do it soon. Don't wait for disaster to strike.

Scripture for Meditation
If you do not do well, sin is lurking at the door; its desire is for you, but you must master it.

GENESIS 4:7

29

The Bigger They Are

In the seminary high school I attended, we affectionately called one classmate Tank, because of his size: well over six feet tall, very broad in the shoulders, weighing more than two hundred pounds. Lumbering down the hallway, he was an impressive sight. Tank's imposing size meant he was the person everyone wanted on his football team. In fact, Tank was a one-man flag football line. He was difficult to get around and he was too strong to push over, so the best tactic was to outsmart him or just get out of his way. We knew that one swipe from his hand could cause great bodily harm. No one ever challenged Tank; we all assumed he was too big and too strong.

Tank's demise occurred in our second year, during a flag football game. Tank was in the middle of a pileup. As everyone else disentangled himself and got ready for the next play, he remained on the ground, holding his nose and sobbing quietly. We all thought he was one step from death. If Tank was crying, things must really be bad. As it turned out, there was only one thing wrong with Tank; he had a bloody nose. The rest of us stood, astounded, watching Tank cry and feel sorry for his little bloody nose. Worse things had happened to most of us during a game, and nobody had carried on as much as Tank.

Reality dawned. As big and strong as he appeared, Tank was really not that tough. When challenged, he could be beaten. That day Tank lost his formidable place on the football field. From then on people challenged him; people knocked him down; the once-indomitable-appearing Tank became just another slab of beef that could be pushed around like anybody else.

■

We give some of our troubles and difficulties a standing similar to that my classmates gave to Tank in our first year. They look so big, so strong, so formidable that we believe there really isn't anything we can do about them. We try a variety of coping strategies: We look for a way around them; we pretend they aren't there; we ignore them as long as we can, hoping they will go away on their own.

Trials, difficulties, and problems are a part of life. Some of them are big and very difficult. As Christians, regardless of the difficulty, regardless of the circumstance or problem, we have power and authority in Christ to confront them. Appearances often count for more than they should. Because something *looks* impossible, we believe it *is* impossible. It isn't until we actually confront a problem and try to do something about it that we discover its true measure.

Sometimes we need help dealing with problems. Difficulties cannot always be overcome solely by ourselves, even if we have faith in Christ and rely on the power of the Holy Spirit. Being members of Christ's body, we rely on one another for help, support, and guidance. Why did Tank lose his invincible stature? Ultimately because a number of people fell on him. Similarly it may require the help of two or three friends to reveal that a problem is not invincible.

Although others can help us, our *own* faith in Christ enables us to confront trials, difficulties, and temptations. When Jairus sought Jesus' help for his daughter, word came that his daughter had already died. Jesus said to Jairus, "Do not fear. Only believe" (Lk 8:50). Jesus says the same thing to us as we confront our serious and difficult problems. "Do not fear. Only believe." Some problems will yield when we finally confront them. Others will require ongoing hard work, discipline, prayer, fasting, and counsel. The apparent size of a problem should not intimidate us. Because we have the same Holy Spirit as St. Paul, we can say, "I can do all things through him who strengthens me."

For Personal Reflection and Response
Are you facing a problem or temptation that seems too big to handle? Talk with a confessor or a trusted friend about getting help. Consider these game plans: confession, healing prayer, changing living patterns, a self-help group, and counseling.

Scripture for Meditation
I can do all things through him who strengthens me.

PHILIPPIANS 4:13

Now when Jesus returned, the crowd welcomed him, for they were all waiting for him. Just then there came a man named Jairus, a leader of the synagogue. He fell at Jesus' feet and begged him to come to his house, for he had an only daughter, about twelve years old, who was dying.

As he went, the crowds pressed in on him. Now there was a woman who had been suffering from hemorrhages for twelve years; and though she had spent all she had on physicians, no one could cure her. She came up behind him and touched the fringe of his clothes, and immediately her hemorrhage stopped. Then Jesus asked, "Who touched me?" When all denied it, Peter said, "Master, the crowds surround you and press in on you." But Jesus said, "Someone touched me; for I noticed that power had gone out from me." When the woman saw that she could not remain hidden, she came trembling; and falling down before him, she declared in the presence of all the people why she had touched him, and how she had been immediately healed. He said to her, "Daughter, your faith has made you well; go in peace."

While he was still speaking, someone came from the leader's house to say, "Your daughter is dead; do not trouble the teacher any longer." When Jesus heard this, he replied, "Do not fear. Only believe, and she will be saved." When he came to the house, he did not allow anyone to enter with him, except Peter, John, and James, and the child's father and mother. They were all weeping and wailing for her; but he said, "Do not weep; for she is not dead but sleeping." And they laughed at him, knowing that she was dead. But he took her by the hand and called out, "Child, get up!" Her spirit returned, and she got up at once. Then he directed them to give her something to eat. Her parents were astounded; but he ordered them to tell no one what had happened.

LUKE 8:40-56

———

30

A Tale of Two Friends

My best friend and I were on the same Little League team. I was the home-run hitter and played shortstop. My friend was our ace pitcher. Most of us looked to him as the team leader. One of his faults, however, was his negative outlook.

He criticized everybody and everything, including his teammates and the coach. As you can imagine, it didn't take long for this attitude to spread to the rest of the team.

My younger brother played for a different team. During one game against my brother's team, the inevitable happened. My brother was called in to pitch, and it was my turn to bat. Because I was older, I expected to connect with his pitches and probably hit a home run. So there we were, brother facing brother. Everybody in the stands and on the teams knew the situation. Needless to say, my sense of identity and manhood were tied up in this little drama. My brother threw a couple of balls, and then I got a good pitch that I hit to deep center field, where the center fielder caught it. I felt a little deflated that I didn't get to base, but this was not a bad outcome. I didn't hit a home run off my brother, nor did he strike me out.

My friend, however, expressed his negative take: it was terrible that I hadn't got a run. Eventually his attitude started to affect me. By the end of the game, which we lost, I was feeling lousy. I was mad at myself, my brother, and the world in general.

Years later another friend of mine, a very encouraging and positive person, would find something good to say about everybody. He encouraged people in small ways, which they found very uplifting and heartening. He was the type of person whom others wanted to be around, because in his presence they found themselves just naturally doing better. His way of encouraging people and his obvious confidence in them brought out their best.

■

My Little League experience was not the fun, positive time it might have been, because of the negative, discouraging attitude my friend brought to the team and to the game. By contrast, the times I spent with my other friend were always good. I remember him fondly; his encouragement and inspiration always called me to be better than I thought I could be.

All of us have the opportunity to affect how others experience life. We can be a source of encouragement or discouragement for them, depending on how we act and talk in their presence. The Letter to the Hebrews tells us that we should be looking for ways to motivate one another toward love and good deeds. This is quite a challenge. Do we have this as our fundamental posture toward others? Do we encourage others and seek to bring out the best in them? Or are we basically negative, seeing only that which is wrong or not right in a situation or person? Do friends, coworkers, and family members experience us as someone who will call them on to their best, or do they think that we will keep them at the status quo?

As we promote the best in others, that which is truly noble in them will be recognized and applauded for what it is. Every day, try to encourage at least one other person to grow in love and to practice good deeds. Not in a holier-than-thou manner, but with a genuine concern that this person does his or her best toward God and neighbor. What a different place the world could be if we would only make the effort.

For Personal Reflection and Response
Take a moment to consider the effects of your actions and speech patterns. Are you someone who builds up or tears down? What type of person do you want to be? Today and

throughout the next week, strive to be encouraging and positive toward others, even those you aren't fond of.

Scripture for Meditation

And let us consider how to provoke one another to love and good deeds.

HEBREWS 10:24

31

You Are What You Eat

When I was young, I used to listen to Saturday morning radio programs before we had a television set. Ovaltine, the chocolate drink mix, sponsored some of my favorite shows. I hated the taste of Ovaltine, but I begged my mother to buy it, because the radio told me that if I drank it I would be strong and competent like my heroes in the programs. Ovaltine was the key to their success whether they were cowboys or commanders of spaceships. A few years later I discovered that Wheaties was the "breakfast of champions." I begged my mother to get Wheaties, so I could be a champion.

Now in my fifties, I find myself examining the nutritional labels of food products and making my choices based on fat, cholesterol, and sodium rather than on taste. I do this because I believe the experts who claim that diet plays an important role in a healthy and long life.

We have all heard people say, "You are what you eat." A doctor friend of mine once told me a story to illustrate this point. A patient in his internal medicine practice came in complaining that both his urine and his stool had turned green. After running some tests, the doctor could find nothing physically wrong with him, so he asked the man about his diet. As it turned out, the man had been, for whatever reason, existing mainly on lettuce for the past month. The doctor advised the man that he was literally becoming what he was eating. If he would stop his all-lettuce diet and eat in a more balanced fashion, his bodily functions would return to normal.

■

What is true of physical nourishment is true of spiritual nourishment as well. We are and will become what we eat. If we eat healthy spiritual food, we will become healthy spiritual people. If we choose to feed upon those things that are of the world, the flesh, or the devil, we become like those things.

To be spiritual champions, we have to eat the food of champions. In the Gospel of John, Jesus invites us to feed upon him as the food and drink of true life. As we receive him in the Eucharist, we become more and more like him. But this saying of Jesus also has a broader meaning for the spiritual life. When we read and meditate upon Scripture or join with Christ in quiet moments of prayer or serve others who are in need, we are eating healthy spiritual food. Consequently we become healthy spiritual people through the power of the Holy Spirit.

Just as it isn't always easy to choose healthy snacks or meals for our bodies, so we sometimes find it difficult to choose healthy foods for our spirits. Unless we are diabetic or under dire restrictions, it is OK to eat a huge piece of chocolate cake and ice cream every now and again; it won't kill us. But a steady diet of chocolate cake and ice cream is certainly not healthy. In the spiritual realm the stakes are much higher. It is not as harmless to say, "I can read a pornographic magazine or go to a sexually explicit movie and it's OK. Just one won't hurt me." Perhaps it won't immediately lead to spiritual death, but it certainly is doing us harm. The way we choose to fill our days—the music we listen to, the conversations we engage in, the thoughts we allow our minds to dwell on, the friends we choose to be with, and how we choose to spend our free time—all can have profound spiritual implications. Virtually every waking moment of the day, we have the opportunity to make a healthy or unhealthy choice.

What habits for healthy spiritual living are we setting in place? With what are we filling our spirits? Are we eating those things that will help us become spiritual champions? Or are we eating things that can kill us?

For Personal Reflection and Response

What makes up your spiritual diet? What do you need to cut out? What do you need to add? Making a spiritual menu for the week can be a fun way to manage your spiritual life. Using the menu form on the next page, check off the "spiritual food group" and the amount of time you will spend with it for each day. (You don't have to partake of everything.) Consider filling out a new menu each week.

Scripture for Meditation

Very truly, I tell you, whoever believes has eternal life. I am the bread of life. Your ancestors ate the manna in the wilderness, and they died. This is the bread that comes down from heaven, so that one may eat of it and not die. I am the living bread that came down from heaven. Whoever eats of this bread will live forever; and the bread that I will give for the life of the world is my flesh.

JOHN 6:47-51

SPIRITUAL MENU FOR THE WEEK OF:

Suggested foods	Sunday	Monday	Tuesday	Wednesday	Thursday	Friday	Saturday
Eucharist							
Personal prayer							
Scripture reading							
Group prayer							
Confession							
Spiritual reading							
Service to others							
Meditation							
Intercession							

32

The Sucker Punch

There we were, standing toe-to-toe, looking fiercely at one another, our fists doubled up ready to fight. Two seven-year-olds, Stan the Bully and I, were squared off over something so insignificant that I can't remember it anymore. At the time it was really important, something worth fighting for. This was my first big fight. I was breathing heavily. My heart was pounding wildly. I fully expected to get the tar beaten out of me. I just wanted to get in a few good licks before the inevitable. I was totally focused and ready.

In the midst of this tension, the eyes of Stan the Bully suddenly got wide, a shocked look came over his face, and he said, "Your mother is going to be mad at you. Look, your shirt is ripped." I fell for it hook, line, and sinker. I looked down to see my shirt. Suddenly lights exploded in my head, and my jaw went numb as the sucker punch landed. By the time I recovered, Stan had already run to the safety of his front porch, taunting me and calling me names. He landed a cheap punch, and I headed home with blood on my lip and humiliation in my heart.

■

Stan the Bully distracted me from the real purpose of the moment, the fight. He was able to turn my attention to something every seven-year-old boy might worry about if he went home with a ripped shirt: "Your mother is really going to be mad."

Motivational experts and leaders in business and

society tell us that it is important for an individual to have a goal or vision for life. It is essential to keep focused on that goal so that other things—which momentarily seem more important—don't distract us and sidetrack us from our real purpose.

As Christians we have a fundamental goal that should pervade all of our lives, that of living fully for God. The devil, our enemy, wants to keep us from achieving that goal; he is a master at knowing exactly what will distract each one of us. Some of us are distracted by material possessions. We believe that we need certain things to be happy and we pursue them rather than God. For others, vanity may be the distraction. Perhaps we are preoccupied with how we look physically or how we dress. A certain type of music can be a distraction. The need to win in any situation distracts some. And others are sidetracked by what other people are doing or not doing. Maybe it is a relationship or a hoped-for relationship. The list can go on and on. The devil knows our weakness. His goal is to keep us from a loving and intimate relationship with our Lord.

Sometimes our distractions come in the heat of focused concentration when we are single-mindedly trying to live for Christ. At other times they come as subtle hints or suggestions that may, at first, not seem too bad. But when we follow them, we find that we have gradually moved away from our focus on Christ and giving attention to his voice. Let's be alert and avoid the devil's sucker punch.

For Personal Reflection and Response

Make a list of the thoughts, actions, and projects that occupied you during the past twenty-four hours and consider how much of your time was spent on distractions. Are you in control of your life or are your distractions in control? Consider what you can do to replace distractions with positive life-giving thoughts and activities.

Scripture for Meditation
Discipline yourselves, keep alert. Like a roaring lion your adversary the devil prowls around, looking for someone to devour.

1 PETER 5:8

Now the parable is this: The seed is the word of God. The ones on the path are those who have heard; then the devil comes and takes away the word from their hearts, so that they may not believe and be saved. The ones on the rock are those who, when they hear the word, receive it with joy. But these have no root; they believe for a while and in a time of testing fall away. As for what fell among the thorns, these are the ones who hear; but as they go on their way, they are choked by cares and riches and pleasures of life, and their fruit does not mature. But as for that in the good soil, these are the ones who, when they hear the word, hold it fast in an honest and good heart, and bear fruit with patient endurance.

LUKE 8:11-15

33

Tongues of Fire

I didn't mean to burn the field, I was just out to have a little fun on a summer afternoon. I had ridden my bike to a favorite creek a few miles from home and spent the afternoon playing in the creek and wandering through the field and little woods that bordered it. I don't really know why I had the matches in my pocket. Why would any ten-year-old boy have matches in his pocket?

As I played in the creek, I noticed the field was covered with wispy, white dandelion fuzz. It seemed as though all of the dandelions had gone to seed at once. For the sake of scientific discovery, I decided to hold a match to the fuzz and see if it would burn. I lit one of my matches and put it on the ground. The white stuff burned, fast. I spent about ten minutes furiously stomping the ground trying to put out the fire I had started. Satisfied that I had controlled my small blaze, I went into the woods to explore a different terrain. As I emerged into the field about forty minutes later, I was startled to find fire trucks, firemen, and people from a local industrial plant standing in the now blackened field. An acrid smell of smoke hung in the air. In a few places the grass still smoldered. As I cheerfully walked across the field, I wondered what could possibly have happened here.

I intended to go right to my bike, but the fire chief headed me off. "Do you know anything about the fire that was here?" he asked.

"No," I replied.

He looked at me a long minute and said, "You didn't start any fires out here?"

I paused, looked around, and said very innocently, "Well, I started a small one way over there." I pointed to a far corner of the blackened field. "But," I hastily added, "I put it out again right away. It could never have done this."

The way the fireman looked at me, I thought I was in big trouble. Finally he said, "Son, don't ever play with matches," and he sent me on my way home.

■

One little match resulted in a very big fire. In fact, that fire could have been a disaster. The industrial plant next to this field was an oil storage area. It wasn't until much later that I fully realized how I had endangered a good part of the city by my foolish play. I was a ten-year-old boy having fun with matches oblivious to the fact that other people were being affected by my small "harmless" act.

We often believe that the small things we say to or about others really don't mean much. We want to believe that our speech is rather harmless. Yet the little things we say often have consequences far beyond anything we actually intended.

God gave us the gift of speech to communicate with and understand God and others. Speech has the potential to be one of life's greatest blessings. With our speech we can build up others, encourage them, let them know that we love and appreciate them. We can comfort others when they are down and help people through tragedies. These ways of using the gift of speech build up the life of Christ within us and others.

We can also just "shoot off at the mouth," taking no thought about what we are saying. We can express bitterness, resentment, hatred. We can display disrespect. We can use our tongues to tear down others, to lie to others, to deceive, to manipulate, to get our own way.

Perhaps no other human faculty is more discussed in Scripture than speech; God is very invested in how we use our tongues. He encourages us to communicate his life, love, and goodness to others through the gift of speech. He warns us that the world, the flesh, and the devil want to communicate their message through our speech. Do I want to use my tongue for God, for truth, for beauty, for love? Or do I want to use my speech for evil and destructive purposes? Every encounter with another person is an opportunity to use our tongues for good or for evil. The choice is ours.

For Personal Reflection and Response

Try to take a few moments every night to reflect on the positive and negative ways you have used your speech that day. Identify some ways to gradually increase positive, encouraging speech with one or two people in your circle.

Scripture for Meditation

The tongue is a small member, but it boasts of great exploits. How great a forest is set ablaze by a small fire!

JAMES 3:5

34

Do You Want Leaves or Fruit?

Every winter on our farm we pruned the grapes, raspberries, and blackberries that needed to be pruned for the fall crop to be plentiful. Even though I did this every year, I was always amazed at how much pruning needed to be done, especially on the grapevines.

A properly pruned grapevine can produce large and healthy grape clusters. Pruning involves cutting the vines back to the main branch, which means discarding vines as long as eight feet. One is tempted to think that the power to bear fruit resides in those long vines; maybe they should be kept. Actually the power to bear fruit comes from the branch. Leaving long vines only takes away from the ability of the branch to produce good fruit. A long, unpruned vine produces only small clusters of hard, sour fruit. A good crop of large, edible grapes requires a serious pruning job every year.

Randall Cirner

■

Metaphorically, it's tempting to equate long, leafy vines with a fruitful spiritual life. We can point to all of the good deeds we are doing, all the prayers we are saying, and believe that these represent our very fruitful spiritual life. But, as Jesus tells us in John's Gospel, it's the pruning that results in bearing fruit. If we are not being pruned back close to the source—the branch—we soon become wild grapevines bearing only small, sour fruit.

Jesus says that the Father, the master Gardener, understands what needs to happen in our lives for us to bear fruit; we must be pruned back. None of us likes to be pruned. It is a painful process. But only through pruning can our lives take the shape that God wants them to have; only through pruning can we bear the type of fruit the Father desires.

If the grapevines I pruned could have spoken before I took the shears to them, they would have been quick to point out how much fruit they had borne the previous year. They would have shown their long, leafy vines and noted how tragic it would be for me to cut them back. They would have complained of the pain of the pruning process.

Without pruning we may extend our leafiness to cover more territory in God's kingdom; at first glance, this may look good. But when the Father comes looking for fruit, all he will find is small, sour grapes. Pruning is a life-long process. It isn't always pleasant. At times it is downright painful. But if we sincerely desire to bear fruit for Christ and his church, we must allow the Gardener to prune us.

For Personal Reflection and Response
How is the Gardener pruning you right now? Are you cooperating with or resisting the process?

This anonymous fourteenth-century prayer cited by St. Ignatius at the beginning of his Spiritual Exercises may help you cooperate more consciously.

Anima Christi
Soul of Christ, sanctify me.
Body of Christ, save me.
Blood of Christ, inebriate me.
Water from the side of Christ, wash me.
Passion of Christ, strengthen me.
O good Jesus, hear me;
Within thy wounds, hide me;
Suffer me not to be separated from thee;
From the malignant enemy defend me;
In the hour of my death call me,
And bid me come to thee,
That with thy saints I may praise thee
Forever and ever. Amen.

Scripture for Meditation
I am the true vine, and my Father is the vinegrower. He removes every branch in me that bears no fruit. Every branch that bears fruit he prunes to make it bear more fruit.

JOHN 15:1-2

35

Live in the Present Moment

I was lying on the dock, totally stressed out. My fiancée, her brother, and his wife were all having a wonderful time swimming, playing Frisbee, and enjoying friendly banter. I was completely focused on my life situation and challenges. I was in my last semester at the University of Michigan, taking difficult courses. I was getting married in a few weeks. My job was not quite paying enough to make ends meet. I was worried about where we would live...So there I lay with my eyes closed in the midst of an absolutely gorgeous July day, anxious about all the things facing me.

"Lord, I need help," I prayed. As time drifted by, I gradually became aware of birds singing in the trees, the penetrating warmth of the sun, the puff-ball clouds slowly moving through the incredibly blue sky, the gentle, rhythmic lapping of waves underneath the dock. Ever so slowly a change came over me. I felt the tension and stress of the past months and my anxiety about the future drain away. Absolutely relaxed, out of pure relief, I laughed quietly. How good it was simply to lie on the dock in the sun and listen to the birds. My stress was gone. Not because the issues had changed, but because I was enjoying the moment I was in.

■

Life is full of stress, challenges, strains, worries, things to do, mountains to climb, rivers to cross, achievements to attain. Many of us approach life with a vengeance; we're goal oriented and focused on those things we believe we must get done while we have time.

As Christians we can struggle with the misguided notion that if we are not constantly doing something to bring others to Christ, or proclaiming the gospel, or defending the faith, we are going to be a failure in the eyes of God. God does want us to be partners in the gospel. He wants us to work with him for the salvation of the world and the transformation of the temporal order. Surely we must concern ourselves with fulfilling our responsibilities and achieving our dreams. But to focus on tasks misses one of the main reasons God created us—simply to be. This is what I realized lying on the dock. I was focused on tasks and was missing the existential joy of the moment, the joy of being in the presence of God and his creation with my friends.

At its frantic pace, the world tells us that success involves "making something" of every moment of the day. We miss much of what God wants for us when we feel so compelled to be doing things that we cannot stop and just be in God's presence or in the presence of other people. It is important for us to learn how to be as well as do.

Let's take time to sit under a tree and watch the leaves drift to the ground. Go ahead and lie on the grass and watch clouds float by. Take a walk in the woods. Spend a couple of hours chatting with friends about life in general. The need for work and serious application to tasks will be there throughout life. Let's also learn to enjoy God in his gifts. Let's prepare now for eternal life where being in God's presence will be the only thing to do.

For Personal Reflection and Response
Choose a day this week when you will take two to three hours and relax in a pleasant environment. Don't try to accomplish anything, just "be" in God's presence.

Scripture for Meditation
Anxiety weighs down the human heart.

PROVERBS 12:25

Martha, Martha, you are worried and distracted by many things; there is need of only one thing.

LUKE 10:41

Therefore I tell you, do not worry about your life, what you will eat or what you will drink, or about your body, what you will wear. Is not life more than food, and the body more than clothing?

MATTHEW 6:25

36

Those Blankety-Blank Markers

I finally had to admit that we were lost. Really lost. We had been walking for hours. The river was far behind us, and we saw no sign of our destination. I had set out with my two sons, ages thirteen and nine, on what I thought would be a five-hour hike to a campground where we would spend a few days fishing.

At the start the trail was well marked. I was confident about finding the campground. But when we reached a small river, the trail markers became confusing. One set of markers went along the river vaguely in what I thought was the right direction. Other markers went up a steep hill and disappeared over the ridge. Nothing in my hiking experience led me to believe that we should take the easier trail. So it was up the ridge for us. Hours later, I knew we had lost the trail. I was tired, and my sons, Tim and Tom, were near exhaustion. I considered our options. We could keep following the trail we were on or backtrack to the river and follow a different trail. I chose to stay on the current trail, hoping that it would soon lead to a major road.

After a couple of hours we came to a fence near a house. As we climbed the fence and walked toward the road, a woman came out of the house and scolded me for being on her property. Then I saw her eyes go to my older son, Tim, right behind me, and then to nine-year-old Tom, right behind him. As she looked from me to Tim, I could see the words die on her lips; by the time she looked at Tom, who was virtually dragging himself out of the woods, her whole demeanor changed. She became very concerned and compassionate. She urged us to sit in the shade. She brought us something cold to drink. She filled our empty canteens with fresh water and tried to give us something to eat. We were miles from the campground, she said, but, yes, other hikers had been confused by those markers. We were not the first group to wind up in her yard.

Knowing my sons would never make it to the campground, I tried to figure where we might camp for the night. A few minutes later the woman said she had called her daughter who would drive us to the campground.

■

The property owner was initially upset, even angry, with me for having trespassed, but she chose to do something else. She had compassion for us and went out of her way to take care of us and make sure that we got to our destination.

We all get lost at times. Sometimes we get physically lost, as I did on the trail. At other times we lose our internal sense of direction and need someone to help us get back on the road to where we want to go. Life's markers can get confusing.

How do you react when someone trespasses on your "property"? What do you do when someone impacts your life in a way you were not anticipating or would rather not have to deal with? Do you ever wish someone would find his own way and stop bothering you with his problems?

We have many opportunities each day to choose to either help people along their way or to shut them out and leave them on their own. Sometimes all it takes is a brief word of encouragement for people to be able to go on. Others may need more of our time, to find out what is troubling them. Perhaps we need to pray for them. Maybe we need to point them in a direction where they can get more expert help than we can provide. God uses these times when people "trespass on our property" to teach us about flexibility and compassion. Rather than viewing someone as an intrusion, we should see him or her as a gift, an opportunity to serve Christ in the person of his brother or sister here in front of us.

Some of us may be so invested in not having other people bother us that we build fences to keep people out. Our fences can be made of various material, such as busyness, self-absorption, superiority, and so on. Jesus made time for those who needed him. He always had a heart for people and was willing to spend even a few moments pointing someone in the right direction. We call ourselves his disciples, choosing to live a life of service similar to his.

Today one of your brothers or sisters may be slightly lost and need a little guidance. Tomorrow you may be completely lost and in need of much guidance. Let's pull down our "no trespassing" signs and our fences and be ready to help one another.

For Personal Reflection and Response
We all have a tendency to build fences to keep others out of our lives. Identify the boards that make up your fence. What can you do to remove some of these boards from your fence?

EXAMPLE: BUSYNESS

Scripture for Meditation
Contribute to the needs of the saints; extend hospitality to strangers.

ROMANS 12:13

Let mutual love continue. Do not neglect to show hospitality to strangers, for by doing that some have entertained angels without knowing it.

HEBREWS 13:1-2

37

The Cherry Thieves

"Tomorrow is the day," I said at dinnertime. "The cherries will be ripe and we can pick them in the morning." I had just come in from inspecting the cherry trees in the backyard in anticipation of our first harvest.

Early the next morning we went out to pick and received a shock. There was not a single cherry left on the trees. I stared in disbelief, wondering who could have possibly cleaned off those trees so thoroughly during the night. As I looked around I noticed a large amount of bird droppings on and around the trees. Ahh. The birds had beat us to the crop.

I was not the only one who had been keeping an eye on the trees: those birds arrived first and got the fruit. This same scenario repeated itself every year until we left that house. Each year I would anticipate the right day for picking the cherries, and every year the birds would beat us by just a few hours. There was a great harvest of cherries awaiting us, we just didn't get there in time.

■

The world, too, has a rich harvest to be brought in for the Lord. Millions of people need to hear the gospel for the first time. Millions of others, although they know the gospel, do not know the personal love of God. They need to experience his love in action where they live and work. John Paul II, in his encyclical *The Lay Members of Christ's Faithful People,* says that the call to work in the Lord's vineyard for the harvest is "addressed to every person who comes into this world." The pope repeats this in an even more profound and striking fashion when he says, "It is not permissible for anyone to remain idle." This encyclical should be required reading for every member of the church. It sets forth in a very direct and profound way God's call to each of us, young and old, rich and poor, with whatever talents we have. All of us are to work with the Lord to bring others into the Kingdom of God.

By the time we reach young adulthood, most of us have

some idea of what we want to do with our lives. Some want to be teachers, or nurses, youth workers, doctors, laborers, or engineers. Some want to work in business or do research. These are all wonderful professions that can bring a great deal of personal satisfaction and also be of service to others.

But consider a key question: Do we see our chosen occupation in the context of working for the Lord in the harvest of the world? Do we hear, feel, and understand the call God gives to each of us, through baptism in Christ, to participate in his work in the world? As lay Catholics we are called to transform this world into a reflection of the coming kingdom of God. Through our actions and our words, we are to be a source of life and inspiration to others who can also then know, love, and serve the Lord Jesus Christ.

The world is indeed ripe for harvest. But as with the cherry trees, it isn't just the owner of the orchard who has an eye on the crop. There are "birds" keeping close watch on the ripening harvest. The world, the devil, the flesh are trying to rob the orchard owner of the harvest that rightfully belongs to him. For some people, we may be their one chance to come into contact with the living God. We may offer their best opportunity to hear about the love of Christ and to experience that love. Let's not pass up the moment. Let's not ignore the call of the gospel. Let's not turn away from the most important thing we could do with our lives.

We aren't all supposed to be priests or religious. As lay people we have a critical role to play in the transformation of the world. Without us, it just won't happen. Our homes, law offices, engineering firms, and business areas are meant to be places where the kingdom of God breaks in upon the kingdom of the world. We are indeed the salt of the earth and the light of the world. We are called to be workers in the Lord's vineyard and to bring in a bountiful harvest. Let's not allow the birds to steal the fruit.

For Personal Reflection and Response

When did you last ask God what he wanted you to do with your life? How can you "work in his vineyard" in your current life circumstances? Is there someone for whom you can be like Christ, bringing the Good News?

Scripture for Meditation

The harvest is plentiful, but the laborers are few; therefore ask the Lord of the harvest to send out laborers into his harvest.

MATTHEW 9:37-38

38

Spiritual Muscles

The athletic department at the university where I used to work has a bench-press club. The idea behind the club is that when a person can bench press a certain weight his name is added to a plaque along with the other people who have lifted that same weight. The minimum qualifying weight is two hundred pounds. I had been eyeing that plaque for some time and finally decided that my name would look good on it. I determined that I was going to press two hundred pounds by my fiftieth birthday. I began my endeavor four months before the big day.

For many years I have followed a fitness routine of running and weight training. I was in pretty decent shape to begin with, but it occurred to me that I would need to change my routine to achieve my goal in the four months I had given myself. Consequently I stopped running and devoted myself solely to weight lifting.

Because of my previous experience, I was initially able to increase the weight fairly rapidly. By the beginning of May I was able to press about 175 pounds. I believed that with redoubled efforts I could make 200 by the end of May. By the end of May, however, I was at 180 and disappointed that I had not met my goal.

As the weights became heavier I would come to a point in my lift where I would "stick." A sticking point is a place where the lifting movement just stops. If you can get past the sticking point, you can continue with the lift. The trainer who was working with me explained that the sticking point was a problem when secondary muscles needed to be strengthened. He suggested that I focus on the development of those muscle groups, because my major chest muscles couldn't do the job by themselves; they needed the support of the other muscles. He also said that fitness experts agree that one should not set a specific date to accomplish a certain weight; just work at it gradually and consistently and it will happen.

I decided to take a different approach and dropped my deadline mentality. I went back to running and set my sights on developing the secondary muscles that would help me get past my sticking point.

■

This little experience taught me not just about physical exercise and weight lifting, but also about the spiritual life. Sometimes in our spiritual development we decide to "major" in a particular spiritual muscle. When we do, we have to be careful not to ignore other supporting muscles. For example, we can't decide to major in prayer and forget about those things that support a prayer life, such as loving service to others or humility or joy. Those things are all necessary if we ever hope to achieve the depth of prayer that we desire. Likewise, if we want to focus on service to others, we must support that service through prayer and prudence or our service will run out of steam.

Another lesson was, in some ways, more important—not setting a deadline. How often do we do this in our spiritual lives? By the end of this Lent, I'm going to be humble. By my twenty-fifth, forty-fifth, or sixty-sixth birthday, I'm going to be a holy and prayerful person. Humility is a worthy pursuit. It's wonderful to be prayerful, and growth in holiness certainly is a high spiritual goal. It is not wrong to have spiritual goals. But we can't set the date for achieving them. Our spiritual growth, as all the masters in the spiritual life tell us, is a matter of God's timing and not ours. We do the things we know we need to do in a consistent, persistent, patient fashion, and God gives us the growth. God is the one who enables us to become more holy, more loving, more patient, more service oriented, more full of faith. By setting our own timetable, we are trying to do it on our own. We behave as if spiritual growth is something we achieve by our human efforts. Yes, it does require our effort, but the growth comes from God. In our desire for spiritual growth, we need to keep two key words in mind: patience and balance.

For Personal Reflection and Response

Are you "majoring" in a certain type of spiritual activity or are you striving for balance?

Do you set subtle and not-so-subtle deadlines for your spiritual development? Try a spiritual activity you haven't done for some time (spiritual reading, intercession, spontaneous prayer, and so forth). Let yourself be stretched by it. Don't stop just because it feels strange, difficult, or uncomfortable.

Scripture for Meditation
While physical training is of some value, godliness is valuable in every way, holding promise for both the present life and the life to come.

1 TIMOTHY 4:8

39

Get the Motorboat

The fishing gear was in the canoe. My friend Bill was already seated in the front. As soon as I stepped from the dock into the canoe, we would be off for a day of bass fishing on Fontana Lake in North Carolina. Canoes are tricky things. You have to be careful to put your weight in the exact center or it will tip. I managed to get one foot into the canoe just fine, but as I moved the other foot forward, I put my weight too far to one side. The canoe tipped. Bill and I and the fishing tackle went into the water.

Some North Carolina good ole boys standing nearby, watching us two young Yankees try to go bass fishing in a canoe, howled with laughter. Bill and I managed to climb up onto the dock and retrieve the canoe and some of our tackle. But most of it was at the bottom of Fontana Lake.

All of this was really my fault. When we arrived at the dock that morning, we had our choice of renting a small motorboat for eight dollars an hour or a canoe for two dollars and fifty cents. I was unwilling to pay eight dollars an hour to go bass fishing. There was no reason why we couldn't canoe around the lake and fish at the cheaper price. So a hundred dollars' worth of fishing tackle now lay at the bottom of Fontana Lake in order to save a few dollars.

We sloshed back to our cabins to change, enduring yet more humiliation from the raucous laughter of our wives. After some fresh hot coffee, we went back to the dock. The owner of the boat rental concession was kind enough to lend us a large treble hook, which we used to drag the lake by the dock. Miraculously, we retrieved our fishing rods. Having most of our gear, we paid eight dollars to rent a motorboat.

Cheaper is not always better. The rental agent knew that. He had tried to talk me out of the canoe and into the motorboat rental. But I had been so confident in my ability to handle the canoe that I had disregarded his advice.

■

Have you ever been tempted to take the economy route in your spiritual life? Sometimes we look at the price Jesus says we must pay and decide it is too steep. We just don't want to give God everything he is asking for. We give him only what we are willing to pay at the time and hold back the rest. Sometimes what we hold back involves personal preferences; we just want our own way. Sometimes we don't want to give up things or actions that are harmful to us or to other people. Do we want to give the Lord all of our thought life or all of our speech patterns or all of our eating or drinking habits? What about giving him our relationships, our time, our future? Maybe we don't want to forgive someone who has deeply hurt us. Perhaps we want to hang on to drugs or some sexual sin. So we pay canoe price and try to navigate life.

We may be able to paddle around for a while, but we will eventually make a false step and find ourselves in the drink. The canoe price does not give us much margin for error.

The motorboat costs more, but it is a much more stable and reliable craft that provides greater freedom of movement. We may be afraid that giving every area of life over to the Lord will restrict us; we won't be able to have fun. Just the opposite happens. We have more freedom, more room to move around. The Lord's intention for us is not restrictive but freeing. He opens new possibilities for us, new freedoms, and a more secure hope and future. Sure, paying the higher price for something seems more difficult when we first shell out the money. But in the end, we are glad we bought quality. Buying cheap usually costs more in the long run.

If you ever go bass fishing on Fontana Lake, I highly recommend that you pay for the motorboat. In your life with the Lord, I highly recommend that you pay the full price.

For Personal Reflection and Response

Are you trying to get away with paying the Lord only the canoe price? What areas of your life do you need to give over to him?

You can give your whole life over to the Lord right now. The following prayer can help you do so:

Lord Jesus Christ, you are the desire of my heart. You are my treasure. I give my life to you completely to love you and be loved by you. Take my life, Lord, and do with me what you will. I give you all I am and all I have. May I never be separated from you. Amen.

Scripture for Meditation

The kingdom of heaven is like treasure hidden in a field, which someone found and hid; then in his joy he goes and sells all he has and buys that field.

Again, the kingdom of heaven is like a merchant in search of fine pearls; on finding one pearl of great value, he went and sold all that he had and bought it.

MATTHEW 13:44-46

40

Read the Signs!

The tent camper was a mess. Food and equipment were scattered around the small interior, the canvas was ripped, the door was wobbling on its hinges. We found the Styrofoam cooler a short distance from the camper.

The bear had dined well that night: ham, a bag of oranges, some potato chips and Twinkies. We were outraged. The animal had plundered our camper, scattered things around, and made off with some of our food. We were going to do something about this!

Some friends and I were camping in the Great Smoky Mountains outside Gatlinburg, Tennessee, and had noticed the signs everywhere that warned, "Keep all food locked in the trunk of your car." Well, we didn't think that applied to all food in all circumstances, so we kept our food in the little pop-up tent camper in which we stored all our equipment and provisions. We slept in tents. The very first night the bear paid us a visit.

After surveying the damage, we marched over to the ranger's house and banged on the door. It was 6:00 A.M. The ranger came to the door, obviously awakened from sleep, his revolver in his hand. We stood there, four scruffy-looking college students, demanding that the ranger do something about the bear. The ranger looked bored and disgusted. "Read the signs," he said. We continued to protest that the bear had made a mess of the camper. The ranger said, "Read the signs." He went back inside and closed his door.

That night we took additional steps to keep the bear out of the camper. We folded it down, put a tarp over it, and wrapped ropes around the tarp. We went to sleep confident that we had things secured. We awakened later to the sound of tearing and ripping. We saw a large black bear systematically shredding the tarp and canvas top on the camper, trying to get at the food. We banged pots. We yelled and screamed and watched with some satisfaction as the bear ambled away. Assessing the situation in the morning, it appeared that putting the top down had resulted in even worse damage.

Once again, we trudged over to the ranger's home, only to hear exactly the same words: "Read the signs."

■

For whatever reason, our group didn't quite believe that the signs meant what they said. We believed that placing the food inside the camper was the same as keeping it locked in the trunk of the car. We found out the hard way that this was not the case. People who knew about bears wrote those signs. We thought we had a better idea, but we paid the price for our ingenuity.

In Scripture, God gives some pretty clear instructions about how we ought to live. There are definite, plain admonitions about things we ought not to do as well as directions for things we should do. We have a choice of either following these directions from God or not. How often do we find ourselves banging on God's door, complaining to him about something that is going wrong? We complain about how unfair it is and demand that God do something to rectify the situation. We demand that he keep the spiritual bears out of our lives. We demand this even though we decide not to obey his signs.

We sometimes believe that we can wander outside of the confines of God's plan for how we should live as Christians and expect not to pay any price for it. After all, why should anything bad or disastrous happen when I am *close* to doing what God is asking me to do? There is something in us that wants to come up with our own approach to doing things. We like to believe that our personal understanding, experience, or creativity can devise a way of living in the world that is just as effective as God's.

Sometimes we think that what is required is too much. "It's ridiculous to expect me to put the food in the trunk of my car every night and take it out again in the morning. That's just too much hassle." In the spiritual realm we can have the same attitudes. "How can God possibly expect me to..."

Sometimes we want to believe that the spiritual signs don't apply to our situation, and we ask God to give us our own personal signs. The park ranger did not go to every campsite each night and ask people if they had remembered to put their food in the trunk. The signs were clear; the expectation was that everyone would follow them. The Holy Spirit knocks at the door of our conscience to point us toward the spiritual signs. It's up to us to respond to his promptings.

Certainly not every bad or difficult thing that happens to us can be attributed to our not acting in conformity with God's will for our lives. But sometimes we do experience the negative effects of not being in tune with God. Some areas, such as illicit sexual involvement, are under our control. We can do something about these situations. Read the signs.

For Personal Reflection and Response
In what areas of your life are you ignoring (or confused about) God's signs? Make one or two new resolutions to better understand and to follow God's directives.

Scripture for Meditation
Whoever gives heed to instruction prospers,
 and blessed is he who trusts in the LORD.

PROVERBS 16:20 (NIV)

Why do you call me "Lord, Lord," and do not do what I tell you? I will show you what someone is like who comes to me, hears my words, and acts on them. That one is like a man building a house, who dug deeply and laid the foundation on rock; when a flood arose, the river burst against that house but could not shake it, because it had been well built. But the one who hears and does not act is like a man who built a house on the ground without a foundation. When the river burst against it, immediately it fell, and great was the ruin of that house.

LUKE 6:46-49

41

Lifelong Consequences

Before the days of self-service, I had a part-time job in a gas station. I pumped the gas, checked the oil, washed the windshield, and generally saw that the customer's car left in better shape than when it came in. One of the people I worked with was a delightful, older guy, who had a ton of stories to tell and always seemed ready to talk about anything and everything.

Early in our acquaintance, he told me he had one inviolate rule: On weekdays he never drank beer before 5:00 P.M.; on weekends he never drank before noon. During the week, at 4:55 P.M., he would say, "I'm going across the street." He went to a beer store and returned in five minutes with a six-pack under his arm. He took the six-pack into the storage room, and between five and six o'clock this guy drank six beers. He repeated this scenario at 11:55 A.M. on Saturdays.

At first I found it rather amusing and somewhat endearing to think that he was so strict in keeping this rule. But in time I noticed that alcohol was his favorite topic. He was always talking about when he was going to drink or what he had been drinking the night before. He talked about the innumerable ways he had found to drink while driving. He was particularly proud of the ingenious methods he devised for hiding his alcohol while on long fishing trips into Canada.

I also noticed that as his appointed drinking time got closer, he became agitated. His nervous habits became more pronounced. He looked at the clock more frequently. He became irritable and short with me and with the customers. God help those who came in just as he was getting ready to go across the street. They got the quickest fill up and swipe across the windshield you ever saw. This man needed his beer. His abuse of alcohol had serious consequences for him, physically, emotionally, and spiritually.

■

When talking about destructive habits or patterns such as alcoholism, we often focus on the moral issue and overlook the physical, emotional, and social effects such things can have on us. Sexual activity outside of marriage, alcohol abuse, and drug use are not only moral concerns. Such behavior can have serious physical, psychological, and social consequences. Sex outside of marriage, for example, is a social issue (how you treat another person, the possibility of pregnancy). It is a physical issue (sexually transmitted diseases, other health problems). It is a psychological issue (lack of trust, guilt, confusing intimacy with sex). The same is true for alcohol abuse and drug use. There are lifelong consequences.

The moral guilt of sin can be dealt with when one truly repents and honestly confesses such sins. But the non-spiritual consequences of sin have no simple solution. You cannot go to a counselor once or twice and have healthy psychological functioning restored. The streets of our cities, as well as clinics and hospitals, are full of people who thought they could dabble in drugs and not get hooked. Pregnancy among unmarried teens is at epidemic proportions. Although sex, alcohol, and drugs are not the only activities with destructive consequences, they seem to be the key issues among young adults today. This is a good time for all of us—of any age—to take a look at how they affect us.

Now is the time to consider what future consequences—not only moral, but also physical, psychological, and social—our current actions will have. God's laws are for our good, not just our eternal good but our present good. Each of us is the only one who can determine what his or her future will be like. It is in our hands.

For Personal Reflection and Response

What consequences have you experienced from engaging in abusive patterns or sinful behavior?

Is there some young person or group of young people who might benefit from what you have to share? Consider writing a brief letter describing your experiences. Include a section giving straight advice to young people.

Scripture for Meditation
While I kept silence [about my sin], my body wasted away
  through my groaning all day long.

PSALM 32:3

42

What's in Your Attic?

Rattle, rattle, rattle, rattle, clunk. Scurry, scurry, scratch, scratch. Silence. I turned onto my right side. Rattle, rattle, rattle, rattle, clunk. Scurry, scurry, scratch, scratch. Silence. I turned onto my left side and pulled the blankets up over my ears. Rattle, rattle, rattle, rattle, clunk. Scurry, scurry, scratch, scratch. Silence. I put the pillow over my head.

This little red squirrel was driving me bonkers. He was in the wooden eaves running alongside our bedroom. It was early fall, and he was gathering black walnuts from around the yard and storing them in his newfound home in the eaves. The squirrel pushed a black walnut along the board until it came to his storage place where it collided with the other walnuts with a clunk. Then with a scratch and a scurry, he scuttled out looking for another nut.

I finally got out of bed and pounded on the wall near the eaves, hoping to scare him away. It did for a while, but he returned and we were back to the same routine. I have no idea if or when this squirrel ever slept. He was constantly on the move. My pounding on the wall did absolutely no good. After enduring days of this, my wife finally stated the obvious, "You need to find the hole and plug it."

The following Saturday I went looking for the little critter's entrance. I found a neat, golf-ball-sized hole, just right for red squirrels and black walnuts, and nailed a piece of plywood into place. The noise from the squirrel ceased and I was able to sleep.

■

Our thought life can often be as troublesome as this little red squirrel. Distractions, negative attitudes, fears, anxieties, and worries may rattle around in our minds as the black walnuts rattled around in my farmhouse. At some point we get frustrated and bang on our mental walls, hoping the thoughts will go away. They may stop for a while but return as noisily as ever.

Sometimes disordered thoughts reflect a psychological difficulty that requires professional help. Most of the time, however, a disordered thought life is the result of a lack of discipline. Some of us have the notion that this cannot be controlled. We believe that whatever enters the mind is just there; nothing can be done about it. We are content to be held hostage by a seemingly independent thought parade.

Others of us deal with unwanted thoughts by beating on the walls of the mind, demanding that the thoughts leave, hoping that shouting, wishing, or forcing will do the trick. Still others take a spiritual route, asking God to take away disordered thoughts, as if it were his responsibility to organize our minds for us. These strategies don't focus on the real problem. The solution to my squirrel problem was to plug the holes that gave him access. The solution to our thought problem is to plug the holes that provide access to disordered thoughts.

What are some of the holes we may need to plug? The media is one potent source of images and ideas that can lead to unwanted or disordered thoughts. What we watch, read, and listen to can create holes through which thoughts of sex, anger, violence, materialism, self-indulgence, fear, and destructive notions of self enter and wreak havoc. What about our choice of friends and topics of conversations? These can promote either a positive or negative mental atmosphere.

Dwelling on negative thoughts can be a manifestation of self-pity. We feel sorry for ourselves so we allow negative images of ourselves or others to dominate our thoughts. This negativity reinforces the belief that we really should feel sorry for ourselves, and the cycle continues. It seems easier to give into self-pity than to deal with it.

Controlling the points of entry to our thoughts takes discipline and work, but the result is a free mind, a mind we can use for things that will build up others and ourselves. We will have more mental energy available for studies, for our work, and for helpful spiritual activity. Let's plug those holes. Give your mind and spirit some peace.

For Personal Reflection and Response

Are you in control of your thought life? Are you filling your mind with harmful material: pornography, sexually explicit music, self-pity, comparing yourself with others? Today is a good day to make a resolution to gain control of just one area. Ask the Holy Spirit to help you.

Scripture for Meditation

Finally, beloved, whatever is true, whatever is honorable,

whatever is just, whatever is pure, whatever is pleasing, whatever is commendable, if there is any excellence and if there is anything worthy of praise, think about these things.

PHILIPPIANS 4:8

Do not be conformed to this world, but be transformed by the renewing of your minds, so that you may discern what is the will of God—what is good and acceptable and perfect.

ROMANS 12:2

43

Accept No Imitations

The time of day was right. A nice natural hatch of flies was taking place on the stream. My casts were passable. Trout were feeding all around me on the stream in western Pennsylvania. But none showed any interest in the dry fly I was using, though just upstream from me, another fly fisherman was regularly netting nice fish.

I continued changing the size and pattern of the fly I was using to no avail. The trout just weren't taking it. Later in the day the other fisherman and I wound up on the bank taking a little break, discussing the wonders of fly-fishing. I mentioned that I was not catching anything, but he seemed to be doing quite well. He asked me what kind of fly I was using. When I showed him the assortment I had tried that morning, he said, "Well, there is your problem. Your flies are not matching the hatch on the river today." He then showed me what he was using and lent me a couple. After that, it was just a matter of time and patience before I began catching fish.

■

As a fly fisherman I am intrigued and fascinated by the fact that fish take an imitation fly when it is presented correctly. Why? Because a well-tied and presented imitation has the appearance of a real fly. The whole enterprise of fly-fishing is based on deception: to make a fish believe it's getting the real thing. One of the best times to be on a trout stream is when a natural hatch is taking place. The trout are less discriminating; they are so busy feeding that they may take even a poorly presented imitation. But under normal conditions, the artificial fly has to be presented just right. It has to drop delicately on the water and float naturally on top. Most important, it has to have a pattern similar to a natural fly; the trout are attracted to pattern. Smart fishermen spend a lot of time studying the stream and the patterns of the naturally hatching flies. Being able to match the hatch distinguishes artful, successful trout fishermen from those who go home empty-handed.

We humans can act like trout—not too bright. In our quests to satisfy our longings and desires, we are often attracted to things that are imitations rather than authentic. Unless we take time to closely examine and discern what is being presented to us, we assume that if it looks like the real thing, it is the real thing. Only after we "bite," do we discover we are hooked on something we hadn't expected.

We all have a God-given longing for love and loving relationships. In our quests for such relationships, we can be fooled into thinking that something that looks like love is love. Sex is an important part of a loving relationship between a man and woman in marriage, but outside of that context it is not the real thing. Many people, including Christians, mistake sex for love. We get into a sexual relationship expecting to satisfy the longing for love and mutual respect only to find we've been snagged by a painful hook. The relationship that began in hope and expectation ends in pain and struggle.

Other longings can succumb to imitations: Alcohol and drugs may look like joy. Lack of discipline may seem like freedom. Thinking badly about oneself may appear to be humility. Judging others may feel like righteous indignation. An abundance of religious activities can look like a deep relationship with the Lord. In all of these, we mistake the pattern for the real thing.

The devil is a master fisherman. He knows how to present imitations in just the right way at just the right time to entice the unsuspecting. He knows how to "match the hatch." He can determine our longings and needs, and he presents something that looks very much like the real thing. Without right judgment and discernment, we will be hooked on the devil's imitations. A hungry fish, however, is less likely to be as discriminating as a full one. If we are already full in the Lord and healthy relationships, we are less likely to take the imitations presented by the devil.

We must be careful to discern what is presented to us and not just grab whatever comes along, even if it seems as if it might meet a deep need. If we are patient, the real thing will come our way. Let's not wind up in the devil's creel.

For Personal Reflection and Response

Try this little experiment. Get a glass of real orange juice and a glass of imitation orange drink and place them next to each other. What differences can you distinguish by looking at them? Is there any difference in smell? Now taste them—the real thing first, then the imitation. Which do you prefer? Which is better for you?

What imitations—for love, for a relationship with God—are you pursuing?

Scripture for Meditation
My child, do not let these escape from your sight:
    keep sound wisdom and prudence,
and they will be life for your soul
    and adornment for your neck
There you will walk on your way securely
    and your foot will not stumble.
If you sit down, you will not be afraid.

PROVERBS 3:21-24

44

Don't Dig Up Those Seeds

When we lived on a small farm, we enjoyed gardening and landscaping. We maintained raspberry and blackberry bushes, grapevines, and an asparagus bed. We planted peas, beans, corn, carrots, potatoes, pumpkins, and other vegetables and fruits.

One of my favorite projects involved planting four hundred pine tree seedlings. My two sons and I spent an entire Saturday putting the seedlings in the ground, close together, near the garden. Eventually we would transplant most of them to other places around the farm.

The growth of plants—whether vegetables or fruit or trees—is a mysterious process. When I looked at my little seedling trees and tried to imagine that these would one day be sixty to eighty feet tall, I had to stretch my imagination. The vegetable seeds I put in the ground didn't seem like much. Often I looked at those seeds and wondered if they would ever become what the photo on the seed packet promised.

While waiting for them to sprout, I wondered if anything was happening beneath the soil. I was tempted to dig one up to inspect it. Was it making any progress? Had it started looking like a green bean yet? I resisted the urge, knowing that digging up that seed would be disastrous; it would interrupt the rooting process and kill the embryonic plant. If I weeded, watered and mulched and left them undisturbed, eventually those little seeds would become exactly what they were supposed to.

◼

Some of us may be wondering whether our spiritual plantings are bearing any fruit. Are we becoming more holy through our fasting, works of mercy, prayer, Scripture reading, and going to Mass? Are these efforts bringing us closer to God? Is any growth happening at all? We may be tempted to examine our lives minutely to see how much we have grown. But spiritual growth is just as mysterious as the growth of seeds, if not more so. As Jesus emphasizes in the Gospel of Mark, the kingdom of God grows seemingly on its own.

Every gardener knows that the seed of the pea contains within itself the code for the seed to become a vine full of peas. It isn't the sun or the rain or the fertilizer that makes peas. Pea seeds make peas. Likewise in our spiritual life, it isn't prayer or fasting or almsgiving that makes us holy, it is Christ's life within us, the presence of his Holy Spirit, that brings about growth in holiness. The other things are critical, because they provide an environment within which growth can take place.

At times, spiritual growth seems to take place in a maddeningly slow fashion. The Holy Spirit works at his pace to bring about our transformation into the image and likeness of Christ. Let's not become discouraged or disheartened if we don't see immediate change. Our problems won't be fixed overnight nor will holiness blossom immediately. God doesn't work that way.

We must resist the temptation to become introspective since introspection can lead to intensity, discouragement, and a focus on self. Our focus should be outward. We should praise and thank God for the life he has already given us and quietly continue those practices that help nurture holiness. Then we must be patient and let God give us the growth.

For Personal Reflection and Response
If you haven't already done so, this is a good time to establish a daily spiritual plan.

How much time can you give to God each day? Use that time to pray, read Scripture, and read some writings on lives of the saints.

Scripture for Meditation
The kingdom of God is as if someone would scatter seed on the ground, and would sleep and rise night and day, and the seed would sprout and grow, he does not know how. The earth produces of itself, first the stalk, then the head, then the full grain in the head.

MARK 4:26-28

45

A Valentine's Day Surprise

Valentine's Day 1970 is forever imprinted on my mind. It's the day my whole notion of marriage changed. Therese and I had been married just a few months and we, along with a number of other newlyweds, celebrated Valentine's Day together.

Someone baked a heart-shaped cake, and we gathered in a candlelit living room of one couple's apartment. An Episcopal priest had been visiting our prayer group. Because we knew him to be a man of wisdom, married and with many years of marriage counseling experience, we had invited him to join our little celebration and say a few words about the meaning of love in marriage. As we gathered that evening, we all expected eloquent insights into romantic love.

The first words out of his mouth were, "The most important thing about each of you couples is not that you are husband and wife, but that you are brother and sister in the Lord." His words turned on a very bright light in our candlelit room. The mood of the evening changed. He went on to explain the profound notion of being brother and sister in the Lord and what that meant for us as husbands and wives and soon-to-be parents.

That evening my wife and I began to look at each other differently. Our marriage relationship took on a whole new meaning for us.

■

Marriage is a wonderful vocation. It is God's gift to the human race and something to be received with great joy. In the unity between husband and wife, the apostle Paul saw the mystery of the relationship between Christ and his church. The church, understanding the abiding presence and action of Christ in marriage, recognizes marriage as a sacrament. The bond and the grace of the sacrament allow husband and wife to support and care for each other, enjoy each other, and raise children for the Lord.

It can be easy to romanticize marriage as we do

around Valentine's Day and other occasions, and it's easy to spiritualize marriage and describe it in deep scriptural and theological terms. But what is day-to-day marriage really like? Do married couples walk around all day thinking about the theological meaning of their relationship? Do they meditate daily on the wonders of romantic love? Certainly if couples do not periodically ponder the significance of marriage and their commitment, they can lose sight of what marriage is all about. If couples do not frequently reflect upon and engage in the activities of romantic love, marriage can become a routine and lifeless experience. But marriage is also a day-to-day experience. Husbands and wives awake each day to live out their commitments to love and serve each other, to help each other grow in holiness. They need to fulfill their respective roles as husband, wife, mother, father. Working, cooking, cleaning, mowing the lawn, changing diapers, driving kids around are many of the necessary tasks that make marriage work day-to-day.

Sometimes it seems like a very thankless task. There are times when you feel misunderstood, mistreated, taken advantage of. But these are elements of real life. This is the stuff out of which saints grow. Some people think that the best way to sanctity is by making a commitment to celibacy, devoting one's time entirely to prayer and meditation. This is certainly one way to sanctification and holiness. But another way, which is equally rewarding, is to be daily humbled and overjoyed by married life. Saints are created by God; they are not created by a certain state in life.

The church needs strong marriages to bring about the transformation of society and the world. As married couples live out their daily lives and raise children for the Lord, the culture will be brought to Christ and he will be manifested in justice and peace. Marriage is a great vocation. Where would we be without it?

For Personal Reflection and Response

Think about the statement, "I married my sister (or brother) in the Lord." Write a list of words that describe how you should or would treat your spouse with the respect due to a sister or brother in the Lord.

Scripture for Meditation

So the LORD God caused a deep sleep to fall upon the man, and he slept; then he took one of his ribs and closed up its place with flesh. And the rib that the LORD God had taken from the man he made into a woman and brought her to the man. Then the man said,

"This at last is bone of my bones
   and flesh of my flesh;
this one shall be called Woman,
   for out of Man this one was taken."

Therefore a man leaves his father and his mother and clings to his wife, and they become one flesh.

GENESIS 2:21-24

———

46

I Want, I Need, Please Send Me...

Dear Mom and Dad,

How are you? I am fine.
If you get this letter before the next laundry exchange, I want you to send me some extra money with the laundry. I have only a couple of dollars left. Also, I need some more athletic socks

because mine continue to disappear. Finally, please send me some banana bread, because I am starving. That's all for now.

Love, Randy

■

What a warm, loving, and informative letter. No? I regularly used to send such letters to my parents when I was away at a seminary high school. My masterpieces of brevity probably saved an entire forest of trees from being sacrificed for paper. My parents, on the other hand, were less than impressed with my communication skills. Until the day she died, my mother referred to these weekly letters as the "I want, I need, please send me" notes. It was true. I was an adolescent boy wrapped up in my own world, thinking about my parents mainly in terms of what they could do for me. I was their oldest son, away from home for the first time (a big change for all of us). They would have been happy if I had told them what was going on with me but I didn't have time for that. I knew what I wanted and needed and that is what I communicated.

Given this attitude toward my parents, it's not surprising that my prayer life took a similar path. "Dear Jesus, thank you for everything you have done for me. I want, I need, please give me as soon as possible. Thank you. Amen." The prayers weren't quite as simplistic as that, but underneath the focus was on me and what I needed from God.

Perhaps our tendency to treat God in this fashion comes from an understanding that he is all powerful and is concerned about our needs, wants, and desires. But even if the things we ask for are good, this approach misses the fact that God wants to have a relationship with us that goes beyond the "give me" stage. He is more interested in a reciprocal communication. This level of relationship can happen only if we set aside our grocery list and seek God for who he is. Yet many of us find it difficult to break out of the "needs" approach. Perhaps we think God will forget about our problems if we don't keep reminding him. Or that he'll assume our needs are no longer important to us and therefore not important to him, either.

Prayers of petition are often easier to pray because they are action oriented. We are busy and active people who often don't feel we have the time to sit and *be* with God, appreciating his beauty, goodness, love, and mercy. The overall point of prayer is not what God can do for us but entering into a relationship with him, a self-giving communion. It takes time to quiet ourselves to pray in this fashion.

Let's begin a new spiritual journey of prayer by focusing on being with him for his own sake rather than for what he can do for us. Let's put away the grocery lists, communicate our love from the heart, and listen to what God has to say about his love for us.

For Personal Reflection and Response
Try writing a letter to Jesus from your heart, telling him about your hopes, dreams, and fears, especially about your relationship with him.

Scripture for Meditation
[Jesus] went out to the mountain to pray, and he spent the night in prayer to God.

LUKE 6:12

47

New Clothes or New Person?

When I was young there weren't many aspects of going to school that I really enjoyed. There was football in the fall and basketball in the spring, but those had little to do with school per se.

But one thing about the beginning of each school year was exciting. My mother would take me downtown to buy new pants and shirts. If I had done my youthful duty during the summer and properly destroyed my shoes, then buying shoes was also on the agenda. I always liked getting new clothes. Putting on something new and fresh made me feel like a different person. These clothes reinforced the idea that this was a new beginning at school. I was older and, one hoped, smarter. When wearing new clothes, I walked a little straighter and tried harder to keep out of dirt and puddles.

Because of these clothes, I felt that something was different about me. But as the clothes lost their newness, it was apparent that the real me was still there beneath that now fading flannel shirt. Clothes didn't make the man.

■

In our Christian walk we can also believe that something is different inside because the outside looks different. If we go to church more often or pray the rosary or help at the soup kitchen, we must be more holy, right? Well, not necessarily. Only when we are different on the *inside* are we genuinely different. As we appropriate the inner transformation found in Christ, our external life changes.

The results of that inner change? We look different, we act different, and we are different on the outside.

In the Letter to the Colossians, St. Paul encourages us to clothe ourselves with certain characteristics (Col 3:12-17). This encouragement is set in the context of Paul reminding us that because we have been changed by Christ, we should take off the old clothing of sin and bad habits; they are the shabby, worn-out clothes that no longer serve our new life. Instead, we should put on clothes that are befitting the life we have in Christ. He is not telling us simply to look more holy, but to be holy in our relationships because we have changed inside. Our relationships need to be different because we are different.

Sometimes we find that these clothes don't fit well when we first put them on. It can be difficult to be forbearing and loving toward someone who refuses to change his or her destructive habits. It is difficult to be gentle with someone who continues to irritate us, to be patient with someone who shows little regard for us. Yet as we exercise these virtuous habits, they reinforce that new inner life; we grow stronger in both the inner reality and its external manifestations. So let's continue to put on these clothes every day. Let's continue to love one another, be patient with one another, be at peace with one another. Not because we want to look good, but because we *are* good in Christ Jesus.

For Personal Reflection and Response

Why do you perform good or virtuous acts: Do you want to look good or do you want your external actions to manifest the inner transformation the Holy Spirit is working in you?

As you meditate on the verse from Colossians, you may feel drawn to grow in a particular virtue. Ask the Holy Spirit to give you the grace to become the kind of person you want to be.

Scripture for Meditation
A God's chosen ones, holy and beloved, clothe yourselves with compassion, kindness, humility, meekness, and patience.

Colossians 3:12

—

48

Hold Your Fire

Good hunters clearly understand that when game is between you and another hunter, you do not shoot. That day, the rabbit was between us. I immediately took my gun out of position but my hunting partner started shooting. He missed the rabbit, but snow, dirt, and debris kicked up all around my feet where the pellets hit. I shouted and backed away. Finally the rabbit was out of sight, and the shooting stopped. I am not sure whether I was more frightened or angry, but I let the other hunter know exactly what I thought of him and his hunting etiquette. He looked at me blankly then belligerently said, "There was nothing wrong with what I did. I had a clear shot. Anyway, you didn't get hit." I knew this was a person I could not hunt with. I said good-bye and walked out of the woods.

■

A dangerous sport, hunting requires both skill and self-control. Basic hunting rules are key: You never shoot at something you can't clearly see. You don't shoot when game is between you and another hunter. You don't take unnecessary risks with a loaded gun. A hunter who takes those risks is a danger to himself and others.

Self-control is a major issue for all of us. Consider our nationwide problem of obesity. Consider the harm people do to one another through ill-advised words and cutting remarks. Consider the growing problem of addiction to cruising the Internet. Unfortunately many people say they are in control when they are not. My hunting buddy believed that he was in control of his shooting, when actually the desire for getting a rabbit was in control of him. Foolish or dangerous behavior, illicit sexual activity, rape, fighting, automobile accidents, and death are regular results of lack of self-control.

But it isn't just "big things" that require self-control. Consider daily relational patterns. In an effort to let a professor or an employer know how smart we are, do we shed self-control and dominate a discussion? In doing so we may show our expertise, but we also make it impossible for others to participate. Perhaps we initiate or spread gossip to others who don't need to hear our tales. In the process, our lack of self-control damages the reputation of another.

What about self-control in the realm of sports? Too often Christians leave their self-control in the locker room. When we lose self-control during competition, we send a negative message to those around us. It takes a great deal of maturity to play our hardest, be competitive, and not give in to urges to say or do things that are illegal or harmful.

In the spiritual life we can be tempted to want to have it all right now. Multiple devotions, prayers, and intense spiritual activity impelled by a desire to be holy *right now* can lead to spiritual burnout, to say nothing of setting a bad example for others. Just because it's spiritual doesn't mean that we don't need to exercise self-control.

Self-control is a fruit of the Spirit. As we practice restraint, we are becoming Christlike in our approach to life and relationships. Eating, drinking, studying, working, engaging in spiritual activities, relating to others—these are all opportunities for us. We can either "let fly" with the whim of the moment, or we can recognize our responsibility to ourselves and to others to exercise self-control.

Just because we see a rabbit doesn't mean we need to pull the trigger.

For Personal Reflection and Response
Are there areas of your life where you lack of self-control? What are the harmful effects of your lack of restraint on yourself? On those around you? Remember that the Holy Spirit is always ready to help you grow in this virtue.

Scripture for Meditation
Like a city breached, without walls,
    is one who lacks self-control.

PROVERBS 25:28

—

49

God Isn't Looking for Candy Bar Wrappers

My wife's arms were wrapped tightly around my neck. We were squished together in a mummy-style sleeping bag that under ordinary conditions was barely big enough for me. This state of physical closeness was not due to marital affection; it was the bear. Two minutes ago, Therese had been in her own sleeping bag in our two-man tent in a park in Tennessee. In the middle of the night, she had crawled out of the tent and walked down the road toward the outhouse.

Suddenly she had seen directly in her path a black bear rattling around in a garbage can. Whirling around, she had run back to the tent. Quicker than I ever believed possible, she was in my sleeping bag with me.

As we lay there, I tried to reassure her that the bear was much more interested in the garbage than in us. This turned out to be a less-than-helpful comment.

Therese said, "Are you sure you didn't pitch this tent over a candy bar wrapper?"

I told her that bears could not smell candy bar wrappers under tents.

"Sure, right!" We spent some time listening, waiting for snuffling sounds outside the tent. Nothing happened. The bear had wandered away, and we finally got back to sleep. But in the morning my wife made me take the tent down and check underneath for candy bar wrappers. There weren't any. To top it all off, after that night my mummy bag never did zip properly.

◼

We all get a little anxious sometimes when we sin. We know that our sin displeases God and can, if unrepented, lead to estrangement from him. As a result, some of us become scrupulous about our lives. We are concerned about the unknown candy bar wrapper underneath our tent. We fear that God may be on the prowl looking for minute bits of "sin" in our lives, so he can take us to task for them.

This is no way to live the Christian life. Some of us worry that any imperfection is a matter for immediate confession. This is not the teaching of the church. Certainly there are serious sins that need to be confessed as soon as possible. But to live in a state of anxiety about small sins or imperfections removes our focus from the larger issue: to recognize and live in God's merciful love.

Scrupulosity is really a way of trying to be one's own savior. We believe that if we try hard enough and do everything just right, God will not find fault with us and we will be acceptable to him. We will "earn" his love and mercy.

More dangerously, scrupulosity promotes worry and anxiety about things that are not there. My wife was worried about a candy bar wrapper that didn't exist. Scrupulosity compels us to worry about what we "might have" done, often confessing sins or imperfections "just in case." We become wrapped up in ourselves, in the "what ifs," to the extent that we cannot see the day-to-day goodness and love of God. Scrupulosity in an extreme form demands that we perform certain duties and responsibilities and be free of imperfection in order for God to find us acceptable. This form of scrupulosity needs to be submitted to a confessor.

Yes, we need to be cleansed of all our sins before we enter heaven. God will do the cleansing. He knows which sins and imperfections are real. Most of all, God loves each one of us here and now, just the way we are, as we strive to live righteous lives for him. As we grow in our love for God, our imperfections often disappear, not because we anxiously focus on them, but because we take our eyes off ourselves and concentrate on the all-powerful love and mercy of God.

Ferreting out candy bar wrappers will not hasten our holiness.

For Personal Reflection and Response
Consider whether or in what ways you are trying to be perfect through scrupulous attention to defects and imperfections. Speaking with a confessor about perfectionist anxieties can bring valuable outside perspective. Make a decision to follow his direction.

Scripture for Meditation
Through loyalty and faithfulness iniquity is atoned for.

PROVERBS 16:6

50

But He Irritates Me

When I was a senior at the University of Michigan, I belonged to a prayer group. Another member of the prayer group irritated me endlessly. Everything he did—the way he dressed, the way he walked, the way he spoke—got on my nerves.

Some of his personal habits I found not just annoying but downright disgusting. I was supposed to praise God with him, sing with him, and generally be a Christian brother to him, but I couldn't get past my constant irritation. I knew something needed to change, and I was getting more and more frustrated.

One day, I complained about this guy to one of my friends who knew him well. My friend said, "Well, have you thought about praying for him?"

"Praying for him! I've been doing nothing but praying that he will change."

My friend looked at me with amusement. "No, that's not what I mean. I don't want you to pray that he will change. I'm suggesting that you just pray for him. Pray that God will bless him and do good things in his life. Pray that he will know more of God's love and abundance. If you pray in this fashion, I think you'll find that things will change."

Well, I wasn't sure that I really wanted all of

135

those good things in this person's life. Not because I wanted bad things to happen to him but because I wasn't sure I wanted wonderful things to happen. Nevertheless, I was so desperate I decided to pray in the manner my friend suggested. I prayed every day for this guy. I prayed only for his good. I did not pray that any of his perceived problems or irritating habits would go away. I simply prayed that God would love him and bless him.

Things changed, but not the things that I thought would change. The person I was so concerned about continued his irksome habits and bad hygiene. But I found that by praying for him, I began to see him in a different light: I was able to relate to him with more brotherly affection and compassion than I had before. Prayer changed something. It changed me.

■

We all find ourselves in situations similar to this. We know people who irritate us by what they do or what they don't do. Some of these irritations are personality differences that grate on us. Sometimes we become annoyed when a person does something we would never dream of doing. Other times we are judgmental toward people because they don't believe the same things we do or act the way we think they should.

No matter what the source of the irritation, our usual immediate response is to want the other person to change the behavior. The focus is on us and what we want, not necessarily on what is best for the other person. This focus leads only to our being increasingly insensitive and intolerant toward those who get on our nerves.

Let's take Christ's view instead. Jesus was, no doubt,

immensely irritated by all that he saw and foresaw in the human race. He prays for us and our good. He loves and serves us rather than works against us. To be his disciples means to follow his example.

For Personal Reflection and Response

What person irritates you the most? Try to pray every day for this person's blessing, for this person's good. Keep at it until *you* change.

Scripture for Meditation

But I say to you, Love your enemies and pray for those who persecute you, so that you may be children of your Father in heaven.

MATTHEW 5:44-45

51

Are You Anchored?

We pulled into the campground on Lake Superior in late night darkness. The drive had taken much longer than expected, and the small campground was already filled. We had no place to put our two tents. After some searching, we found the "perfect" place, a bluff overlooking the lake. We would have a great view and would catch the breeze off the lake.

Chris and I set up the tents, securing them with small metal anchors while our wives unloaded the station wagon. After everything looked ship-shape, we cooked a much-longed-for dinner over the fire. It was an idyllic picture: a million stars in a black sky, the northern lights flickering in the distance, a gentle breeze, waves lapping on the shore, a handsome fire shared with good friends. Long after midnight we finally crawled into our tents, exhausted but content.

As I lay there I noticed the wind; the sides of the tent were no longer moving gently in a breeze but were taut. A bit anxious, I convinced myself that the tent was secure and drifted off to sleep.

But within two hours both tents had collapsed and our equipment lay strewn around by the lake winds. In the dark we couldn't gather everything, so we quickly secured what we could and spent an uncomfortable night in the car.

Daylight finally arrived, allowing us to assess the situation. The wind was still blowing fiercely, making it impossible to put the tents back where they had been. Instead, using ropes, we anchored the tents to some sturdy trees in another part of the campground. This was the only way we were going to survive that wind. The small anchors we had used the night before were inadequate.

■

In our personal lives when things are calm and peaceful, we don't need to have our "tents" solidly anchored. However, no ordinary anchors will do when the winds blow. We need to know that we are secured to something that isn't going to move. God has provided us with anchors that stabilize our lives and prevent us from being tossed around: faith, hope, and love, the three theological virtues. Through the Holy Spirit these virtues direct our lives toward God and keep us secured to him.

To be anchored in faith means that we rely on God's word to us in Scripture and in the church, which proclaims that he is the one, true God, the Savior of the world, trustworthy and reliable in all that he has said.

When life gets tough, we need not worry about whether God knows what is happening to us, because faith tells us that he is with us and he cares about us. By faith we know he is watching over us; we can rely upon his presence and his care for our lives.

We are anchored by hope, because we anticipate and long for eternal life. We are confident in our expectation of a good future because God has promised it. Our hope is not without basis, because we know that God has been faithful in the past to our forebears in the faith. We have seen the ultimate fulfillment of hope in Jesus' own resurrection from the dead. We see how God has been faithful to us personally in the past. So we are people of hope who do not lose heart when storms rage around us, when the winds blow and our tent seems to be at the breaking point. We know that we can weather the storm, that calm will return, and that we will be at peace.

The virtue of love moves us toward God for his sake and not just for what he can do for us. We know that we love God because we have first known his love for us. We love him completely with our wills, our minds, and our emotions. God's love is steadfast. In the midst of our darkest moments, God's love is present with us. The knowledge of that love anchors our lives in times of great distress. Christ hanging on the cross indicates that, indeed, God's love for us is beyond measure, beyond expectation, beyond our wildest imaginings.

So when life gets confusing, complicated, stressful, or downright horrible, let's remember that we are anchored to faith, hope, and love. We don't have to be blown away by the storms of the world, the flesh, and the devil. When these winds pick up, and we feel as if we are not going to make it, we should check our ropes. We are firmly tied into Christ, and nothing can move us from our relationship with him.

For Personal Reflection and Response
How well do you live in faith, hope, and love?

In which of the three virtues do you most need to grow? Which virtue takes second, and then third priority? To begin a journey of growth, read prayerfully the Scripture passages cited below.

If you want to know more, the new *Catechism of the Catholic Church* has an excellent section on each virtue.

Scripture for Meditation
Faith: Hebrews 11
Hope: Hebrews 6:16-20; Hebrews 10:23; Romans 5:1-5
Love: 1 Corinthians 13

52

Under the Lilacs

My mother's parents operated a small fruit farm in western Michigan. I loved going there as a boy. It was peaceful and relaxing. I wandered through the orchards of apples and peaches, swam in the small lake across the road, and explored the barns. Large elm trees lined one entire side of the road on which the farm was located. My brothers and I spent hours climbing those huge elms.

My favorite place, however, was a large stand of lilac bushes. Old and stately, they formed an archway under which I could walk. In late May and early June, when the lilacs blossomed, I sat in the little tunnel and let the lilac scent and the cool breeze envelop me. My lilac stand was more than a good place to sit and reflect; it was also a place to hide when I had done something wrong and adults were looking for me.

At the end of our visit, it was always difficult to leave the farm. I dreaded returning to normal life and activity—school, chores, my paper route, and the other responsibilities that awaited me back home. Yet I knew I couldn't sit under those lilacs the rest of my life. They provided a brief respite, a time to relax and get refreshment to tackle anew my boyhood responsibilities.

■

The Christian life was never meant to be one long retreat. Peter, James, and John, who accompanied Jesus to the top of the mountain of Transfiguration, were indeed fortunate and blessed to be present with Jesus at that time. It was such an exhilarating experience; the Gospel of Matthew recounts that Peter wanted to build some tents and settle in (17:4). Peter didn't get his wish. The brief interlude of peace, tranquility, and transcendence passed, and the group had to go down the mountain to face reality. Jesus had a mission from his Father that required him to spend long hours teaching, preaching, and healing.

The gospel makes demands on us as well. The demands of our daily responsibilities as students or employees, the demands of being a brother or sister in the Lord to others, the demands of bringing the life and love of Christ to those who don't know him or experience him. In spite of what we might desire, we don't have the luxury of spending most of our time enjoying the quiet delight of prayer, Scripture reading, and meditation.

Rather than pursuing good feelings, we must pursue love of one another. How can we serve one another, forgive one another, help one another? How can we serve not only our families but also people in the neighborhoods and cities in which we live. All around us are God's children in need of a kind word, a supporting hand, or a listening ear.

How can we encourage others as they try to break out of bad habits and patterns? How can we pray attentively and faithfully for the needs and concerns of others?

There are numerous ways to fulfill the demands of the gospel in the world today. There will be plenty of time for lying under the lilac bushes in peace and tranquility. Right now, there is work to do in the vineyard.

For Personal Reflection and Response

How are you living out the practical demands of the gospel?

Identify a person or situation you can serve with your time and resources. For example, consider whether you can work at a soup kitchen, mow someone's lawn, or visit someone in the hospital or nursing home.

Scripture for Meditation

For we are God's servants, working together.

1 CORINTHIANS 3:9

Brothers and sisters, do not be weary in doing what is right.

2 THESSALONIANS 3:13

We must work the works of him who sent me while it is day; night is coming when no one can work.

JOHN 9:4